The Battenkill

Books by John Merwin

Stillwater Trout (ed., 1980)
McClane's Angling World (ed., with A. J. McClane; 1986)
The Compleat McClane (ed., with A. J. McClane; 1988)
John Merwin's Fly-Tying Guide (1989)
The Compleat Lee Wulff (ed., with Lee Wulff; 1989)
The Compleat Schwiebert (ed., with Ernest Schwiebert; 1990)
Salmon on a Fly (ed., with Lee Wulff; 1992)
The Saltwater Tackle Box (1992)
The Freshwater Tackle Box (1992)
Streamer-Fly Fishing (1992)
The Battenkill (1993)
New American Trout Fishing (1994)
Contributing Author:
The American Fly Tyer's Handbook (1978)
Waters Swift and Still (1982)
McClane's Game Fish of North America (1985)

The *Battenkill*

JOHN MERWIN

AN INTIMATE

PORTRAIT

OF A GREAT

TROUT RIVER—

ITS HISTORY,

PEOPLE,

AND FISHING

POSSIBILITIES

LYONS & BURFORD, PUBLISHERS

PRINTED IN THE UNITED STATES OF AMERICA

DESIGN BY HEIDI HAEUSER

10 9 8 7 6 5 4 3 2 1

ALL PHOTOGRAPHS BY JOHN MERWIN

Library of Congress Cataloging-in-Publication Data

Merwin, John.

The Battenkill: an intimate portrait of a great trout river—its history, people, and fishing
possiblities/John Merwin: photographs by the author.

p.   cm.

Includes bibliographical references and index.

ISBN 1–55821–208–6

1. Fishing—Batten Kill (Vt. and N.Y.)—History.   2. Batten Kill (Vt. and N.Y.)—History.
3. Natural history—Batten Kill (Vt. and N.Y.) I. Title.

SH555.M47   1993

799.1'755—dc20

93–11361

CIP

*For DICK FINLAY
and BILL HERRICK,
two friends
who've helped
a great deal...*

Contents

Acknowledgments

Many Battenkill-region librarians endured my nagging questions over several years and were unfailingly helpful. My thanks to the staffs of libraries in Cambridge, Greenwich, and Salem, New York. Also to Gail Rice and staff at the Mark Skinner Library, Manchester, VT, and to Gail Baumgartner at the Dorset, VT, Library. Mary Lou Thomas at the Canfield Library in Arlington, VT, was especially helpful, as was Mary Bort of the Manchester, VT, Historical Society, and Alanna Fisher at The American Museum of Fly Fishing. State fisheries managers in both Vermont and New York provided access to their files, for which thanks to Ken Cox and Bill Miller respectively. Robert Page and staff at the Washington County, NY, Planning Department also provided valuable information.

I've shared the Battenkill with many fishermen over the years, some of whom have become good friends and deserve thanks for ideas shared when the trout weren't taking. Thanks especially to Dick Finlay, Bill Herrick, George and Mary Ann Schlotter, Richard Norman, James Woods, Landy Bartlett, Bruce Bowlen, and Buzz Eichel. Thanks, also, to my family—Martha, Emily, Jason, and Sam—for their support and endurance through yet another of John's books. Finally, a heartfelt thanks to Nick Lyons, my editor and publisher, for his insight and patience.

I extend these acknowledgments knowing full well that each person I've mentioned will probably find one or more statements in this book with which he or she disagrees. Any and all errors or omissions are strictly my own.

The natural historian is not a fisherman who prays for cloudy days and good luck merely; but as fishing has been styled "a contemplative man's recreation," introducing him profitably to woods and water, so the fruit of a naturalist's observations is not in new genera or species, but in new contemplations still, and science is only a more contemplative man's recreation.
— HENRY DAVID THOREAU
A Week on the Concord and Merrimack Rivers, 1849.

Introduction

*T*his is not the book I expected. I was going to write a nice little book about the Battenkill full of folksy fishing yarns and big ones that got away. At the same time I set out to find just what it is that makes the Battenkill Valley such a pleasant place. This became a complex and difficult question, and as I pursued the answer, the river's trout fishing seemed less and less important. Partly because of some odd antipathies that date back for two centuries and more along the border of Vermont and New York, there are no published regional histories that transcend political boundaries. There's also no modern, well-researched history of the state of Vermont, nor did I encounter one covering eastern New York. There are instead the back rooms of local libraries and historical societies where bits of regional history are to be found amid reams of genealogy, old church records, and gloriously bound, nineteenth-century accounts of towns and counties that are so devoted to past heroics that such facts as are presented become questionable.

The river's name is a good example, and one might suppose such a thing to be relatively simple. But not only is there little agreement as to the origin of the name Battenkill, there's also little modern agreement as to its spelling. Various area newspapers use either Battenkill or Batten Kill or sometimes even BattenKill. State fisheries agencies in Vermont and New York presently seem to prefer Batten Kill as two words, but other agencies in the same states use the one-word form. Kill, of course, is the Dutch word for river or stream and is common in much of interior eastern New York that was first explored by the Dutch starting with Henry Hudson in 1609. Of the many "kills" up and down the Hudson River valley and elsewhere, some are traditionally spelled as one word; others as two. There seems to be no consistency from one to another, and there's as least as much historical precedent for the one-word form as for any other, so that's what I've used.

The word "batten" is another problem. Esther Swift, in her 1977 book *Vermont Place Names*, writes that batten is a contraction developed from the name of an early settler near the Battenkill's Hudson River junction; Bart's Kill thus becoming Battenkill, which seems awfully farfetched. Batten in archaic English means to fertilize or enrich, and that explanation was offered by one nineteenth-century historian. But I don't find that very satisfying either. Others have simply insisted that Batten was a surname, without being able to specify just whose name it was.

The most satisfactory answer I obtained came through a second-hand inquiry made to some researchers at the New Netherlands Project at Albany, New York, where work is underway at translating archaic Dutch manuscript materials from the Hudson River region. Here one person suggested that batten was similar in origin to the word batavia, which is a general reference to people of the western-European lowlands that eventually became Holland. There is a Batavia, New York, as well as a Batavia Kill. In that case, Battenkill literally translated becomes "river of the Dutch," which I believe is most logical and reflective of the history of its lower reaches.

There have been Indian names as well, and the one most commonly cited is Ondawa, which is Iroquoian. One writer has given this to mean "white stream," but "country of rounded hills" or words to that effect are probably more accurate. Ondawa was frequently used by romantic nineteenth-century angling writers, and several, widely separated valley farms are called Ondawa Farm; each, I suspect, unknown to the others. My favorite Indian name is a little-used tongue-twister: "Tyetilegogtakook," which is a Mahican name meaning country around the river of toads. Thousands of common toads migrate to the river's many quiet backwaters for mating and egg-laying in early spring, where the noise of their trilling and chirping often drowns the noise of the river itself. The Mahicans were the

Battenkill's native people, and of the river's many names, theirs was the most descriptive.

I have supplemented the text both with endnotes and a long bibliography. By this it might be inferred that I am some sort of historian or scholar, but I'm not. I am a fisherman, often curious, who occasionally writes about things. I have included these details because of my own frustration in tracking down information about the Battenkill, which is fragmentary and widely scattered. If nothing else, this book's bibliography will provide a starting point for others in future years.

My discussion of the Battenkill is arbitrarily and strictly limited to the valley itself; major historical events that occurred nearby — even just over one hill or another — are considered little, if at all. In a broad historical context, this can be very misleading, so consider yourself forewarned. For example, the American Revolution is almost absent from this book because there were no important Revolutionary War events in the valley *per se*, even though such things as British General John Burgoyne's defeat and surrender at Saratoga took place quite nearby.

Much of the upper valley was settled during the late eighteenth century by people from western Connecticut. I also come from a venerable western-Connecticut family, but we didn't settle here until two hundred years later, after making sure it was safe. I mention this by way of pointing out that while the valley is pretty and pastoral in the extreme, it can also be very parochial in the manner common to small towns everywhere, and most especially in Vermont. I've only lived here for twenty years or so and thus make no claims to being a Vermonter. All my children, however, are Vermonters born and bred. Maybe. At this my old neighbor will lean out the window of his pick-up truck and give me a wry smile. "Maybe so, John," he'll tell me. "And maybe not. My cat had kittens in the oven, but that don't make 'em muffins."

That's the way it is. Along the Battenkill.

—JOHN MERWIN
Dorset, Vermont
February 1992

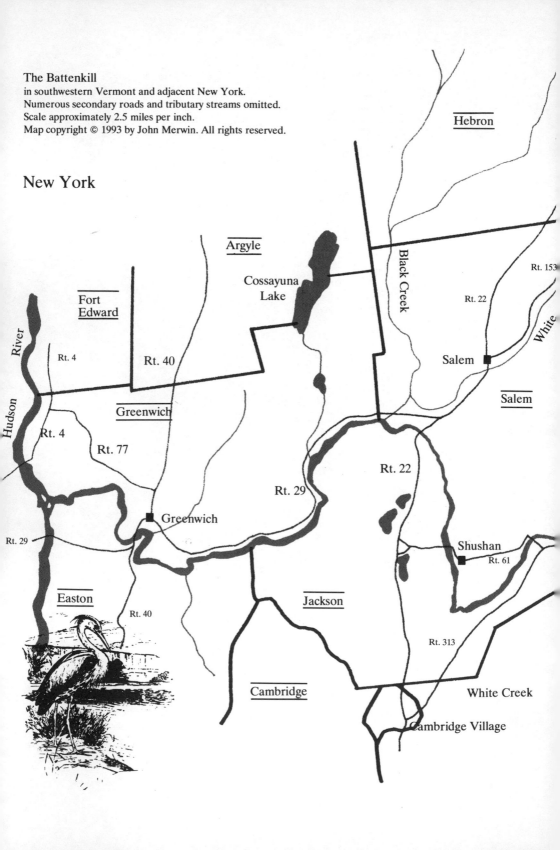

The Battenkill
in southwestern Vermont and adjacent New York.
Numerous secondary roads and tributary streams omitted.
Scale approximately 2.5 miles per inch.

New York

Hebron

Argyle

Cossayuna
Lake

Fort
Edward

Black Creek

Rt. 153

Rt. 22

Rt. 4

Rt. 40

Hudson River

White

Salem

Rt. 4

Greenwich

Salem

Rt. 77

Rt. 29

Rt. 22

Greenwich

Rt. 29

Shushan

Rt. 61

Easton

Jackson

Rt. 40

Rt. 313

Cambridge

White Creek

Cambridge Village

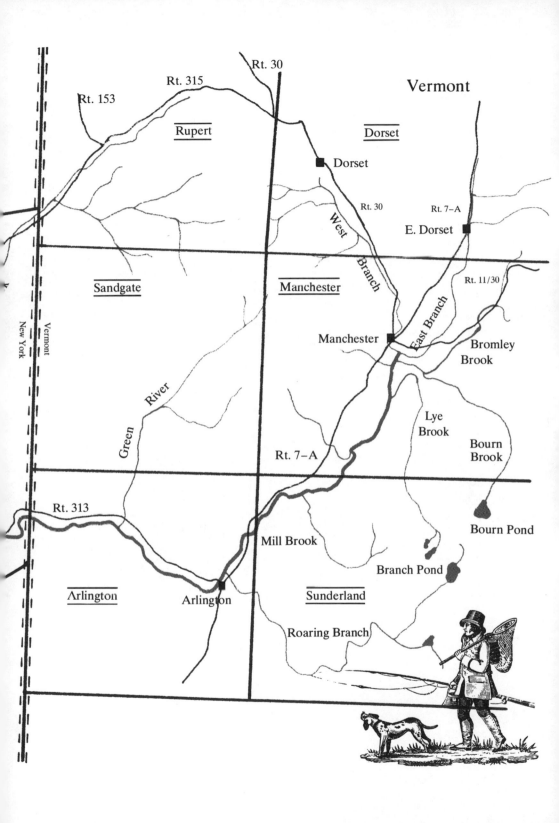

CHAPTER 1

Along the Battenkill

*T*he old woman was bent over in the riverbank bushes, one hand darting back and forth like a little bird along the ground as she picked some small, blue violets. Eventually she stood up, first looking at me as I quietly fished in the lower Battenkill River near Shushan, New York, then staring at my parked car with its green-and-white Vermont license plate.

"You're one of those nasty Vermonters," she said, speaking just loudly enough to be heard over the gently rippling water. She bent back to her flowers.

"Hey, lady," I said, trying to sound injured. "That was over more than two-hundred years ago!" I was referring to the border disputes between Vermont and New York that took place before the American Revolution, one outcome of which was the outright theft of thousands of New York acres by Ethan Allen and his cronies in the name of Vermont. A theft, at least, in New York eyes. By immediate inference, those eyes were hers.

"No, it wasn't!" she said. She sat facing me on a rock; eyes defiant, jaw tight, violets clenched in one wrinkled fist.

It had been a while since I'd seen a rising trout, so I slowly reeled up my fly line and waded over to the riverbank, where I sat on a rock a few feet from my antagonist. She remained motionless, her expression fixed. I tried smiling, but there was no smile in return. Her straw hat was held on her head by a blue scarf knotted under her chin, which led me on a different tack. "Nice scarf," I said. "Matches your violets." She turned her head to look out over the river, having none of my fancy talk.

"You can't possibly mean," I asked, "that all Vermonters are rotten because of what Ethan Allen did or didn't do around here two-hundred years ago?"

"That's exactly what I mean," she snapped. "You're all alike, and it's *still* going on!" As it turned out, she had a long list of problems, foremost of which was her having hired a nearby Vermont firm for some landscaping work that apparently wasn't done properly and on which the firm refused to make good. My sympathetic ear also heard stories of rude trout fishermen blocking her driveway with their parked cars and of canoeists and inner-tube floaters coming downriver from adjacent Vermont and leaving garbage on the riverbank where she liked to pick wildflowers. I finally achieved some minor grace by changing the subject, knowing just enough natural history to comment intelligently on the prevalence of indian pipe — a kind of fungus with plantlike stalks — near this section of the river in June. We talked about plants and wildflowers for some time before I had to leave, ultimately gaining her terse acknowledgment as one of the few nice Vermonters she'd met.

Old grudges die hard in rural country. In the Battenkill Valley of southwestern Vermont and adjacent New York there are still echoes of the half-mythical Allen and his Green Mountain Boys, who were in fact a handful of arrogant tavern drunks bullying New York settlers along the border both before and shortly after the American Revolution. Their abusive tactics have become heroics in modern legend, an attitude reinforced by writers such as the late novelist Dorothy

Canfield Fisher, who lived and wrote in Arlington, VT, which was Vermont's revolutionary-war capitol and is where the Battenkill crosses into New York. She once described some young Arlington men going to the annual Washington County (NY) fair in the 1940s, where, fortified with beer drunk along the midway, they punched a few New Yorkers for the hell of it. She wrote this off as youthful exuberance and noted that the same young men wore their bruises proudly home to Arlington, just like old Ethan.

Such attitudes have even extended to the river's trout fishing, which has been extensively promoted since the upper valley in Vermont first gained prominence as a tourist area during the 1850s. In 1937 the now-defunct *Washington County* [NY] *Post* offered this wry editorial on Vermont's stocking of trout in the adjacent upper river:

> Bennington County [VT] streams will shortly receive 70,000 trout from a Bennington fish hatchery. Planting of these young fries [sic] will be done at intervals. A nice feature of this activity is that 20,000 of them will be gently dropped into the Battenkill. This is the same Battenkill that flows near Shushan and comes even closer to Cambridge. The question is will the trout cross the state line or have they been trained to stay in Vermont? If they are good travelers it should be no trick to catch some of them in New York. Twenty thousand trout can't all be Republicans.[1]

The Battenkill's wide reputation as a trout stream depends as much on the surrounding scenery as on the fishing itself, which is often difficult. Several small tributaries gather at Manchester, Vermont, in the shadow of 3,816-foot Mount Equinox, from which the river flows some fifty miles through southwestern Vermont and adjacent New York to its Hudson River junction at Clark's Mills near Schuylerville and Saratoga. Despite the recently increasing development of its upper valley, the river remains remarkably pastoral. Its gentle, clear flow meanders through lowland meadows surrounded by rolling green hills. There are quiet villages with country inns, white church spires, and covered bridges. It is a calendar cliché come to life.

It's also a mundane place, actually, where nothing much ever happens. Notes of rummage sales, church suppers, and cub-scout meetings dominate the local newspapers, sharing space with occa-

Village green; West Arlington, VT. Norman Rockwell's former home and studio is at left.

sional news of a new town truck, last night's chimney fire down the street, or the capture of a large brown trout from the river itself. Life here is so indeed plain that the artist Norman Rockwell, who lived and painted near the river at Arlington from 1939 to 1953, became internationally famous for his dozens of *Saturday Evening Post* covers showing his ordinary neighbors doing ordinary things.

It is perhaps that sense of the commonplace that is so remarkable — so uncommon — to those who travel the valley for the first time. I have often taken visitors to the village green at West Arlington on Route 313 near the New York state line, for example, and walked with them over the red covered bridge that spans the Battenkill, and strolled under the towering sugar maples bordering the narrow dirt lane. There are a few old farmhouses here, immaculately white with green-shuttered trim, a small white church, and a grange hall with an open picnic pavilion. Neighborhood children will be splashing in the deep pool under the bridge on summer afternoons, or — if it's an evening walk — we may see a solitary fly fisherman standing hip-deep in dark water, magically unrolling a bright yellow line through the air and toward the far bank where trout rise gently in green shadows.

My guests invariably remark that the scene looks like something out of a Norman Rockwell painting, sweetly sentimental but too good to be true. It *is* something out of Rockwell, I answer, while pointing out the late artist's home and studio only a few hundred feet from the covered bridge. Nor is the image confined to Rockwell's work. If our tour continues downstream through the rolling farmscapes of Salem, Jackson, Easton, and Greenwich, New York, exclamations about a "Grandma Moses landscape" are equally inevitable. Here there's more open farmland than along the upper river, and the scenery does indeed look just like many of the late artist's bucolic primitives. Anna Robertson Moses was born near the lower Battenkill at Greenwich (locally pronounced GREEN-witch) in 1860 and eventually settled in the nearby town of White Creek. Her work was discovered on display in an area drugstore by Louis Caldor in 1938; major exhibitions quickly followed, and this unassuming country woman quickly became the best-known name in American folk art. The countryside she painted has changed little since her death in 1961. Cattle still dot the open fields; the same streams still flow under the same covered bridges; and farm families still gather in celebration of Thanksgiving

Rolling farmscape typical of the lower Battenkill in New York.

and Christmas. There is still a childlike innocence in the modern landscape, just as there was in hers. A large body of her work has been collected by the Bennington (VT) Museum, which is open to the public all year, but the rural Americana it so vividly portrays is still best seen in the land itself.

To the extent that it satisfies a yearning for small-town nostalgia, the valley is complete. Its little towns and village districts offer a strong sense of community and stability, an umbrella under which life is lived deliberately and where the essential facts of life are confronted on the sidewalk daily for lack of any other diversion. They are still what Sherwood Anderson, the late midwestern novelist, called an "invisible roof," beneath which

>...boys and girls were born, grew up, quarreled, fought, and formed friendships with their fellows, were introduced to the mysteries of love, married, became the fathers and mothers of children, grew old, sickened, and died...

This sounds like a blueprint for Rockwell's work, which it was, but small-town life here as elsewhere is not always the Warm Fuzzy so cheerfully shown by Rockwell, Moses, and others. There's a certain lack of privacy in an area where everyone's business is well-known to everyone else. There are also occasional fits of mean spirit from narrow minds resistant to change, coupled with the pressures toward conformity endemic to small towns. In those river towns such as Dorset and Manchester, Vermont, that have become sufficiently affluent to care about their looks, municipal design-review boards actively work to ensure that village clapboards are painted the right *shade* of white. And speaking of white, there are also occasional flashes of bigotry in an area where racial minorities are conspicuously absent and where old-line golfing clubs are WASP-ish to the point of self-parody.

Through all of this runs a trout stream. The Battenkill is the only common thread linking the old-line resort communities of Manchester and Dorset near its headwaters to towns that become increasingly rural as one progresses downstream toward the Hudson. The river itself is as unusual as the small towns along its banks, being cleaner and more free of dams now than at any time in the past two centuries. Its purity is a social accident; nineteenth-century milling and manufacturing that were sources of virulent water pollution have gradually given way to tourism as an economic base for the upper valley, and the river has gradually cleansed itself as a result of this change. Because the Battenkill offers exceptional habitat for wild trout, both New York and Vermont curtailed stocking of hatchery fish in much of the river after the mid-1970s. Streambred brook and brown trout are relatively abundant, although their numbers are depressed by creel limits that are overly generous given the river's wide reputation and intense fishing pressure.

The river begins as two branches in Dorset. The East Branch starts as a few boggy, side-hill spring seeps about eight miles north of Manchester along route 7-A. By more local reference, that's a few yards south of Harold Beebe's old sugarhouse. Fishing between here and Manchester is difficult because of thick brush growing to the water's edge, but can also be productive as a result. There is no marked access, which is best obtained by the railroad tracks adjacent to the stream. The East Branch flows south through East Dorset, the birthplace of Bill W. (William G. Wilson), who was the co-founder of Alcoholics Anonymous and who is buried nearby. The old Wilson family hotel in the village has recently been run as an unadvertised rooming house for those following Bill W.'s famous Twelve Steps.[2] Just above Manchester proper, an old state-owned dam on the East Branch creates what's locally called DuFresne Pond, which is annually stocked with brook trout by Vermont and which is the only location on the entire river that offers ready public access for handicapped anglers.

The East and West branches are separated by a high ridge, which is part of the north-south trending Taconic Range. The West Branch begins immediately south of Dorset village[3] on Route 30, a quiet enclave for old money since the Civil War. Here the members-only Field Club boasts what's arguably the country's oldest nine-hole golf course with local course maps dating to 1886. Numerous springs high in the adjacent Taconics as well as in the valley floor feed the West Branch, which gathers in a large, cold-water marsh visible from Route 30 south of the village. Wildlife, brook trout, and numerous rare plants are abundant here, although public access is almost nonexistent because of surrounding private property. The Dorset RV

Dorset Village, VT. —just one white clapboard after another.

Park on Route 30 between Dorset Village and Manchester borders a portion of the marsh and offers campsites as well as hook-ups for recreational vehicles.

Dorset Village itself is quaint with a capital Q. There are perhaps more linear feet of white-painted clapboards per capita here than anywhere else in Vermont. Three venerable country inns and an excellent summer theater are within shouting distance of the village green, over which Peltier's General Store presides like a dowager queen, her green-awning eyelids drowsily shading geranium window-boxes from the summer sun. Proprietor Jay Hathaway stocks a wide variety of gourmet foods for his numerous upscale customers —

including exotic coffees, both whole bean and freshly brewed — which occasionally produces a gentle collision of cultures. While getting my own coffee and newspaper here early each morning, I sometimes encounter a roughly clad logger or trucker doing the same thing. Hearing one of these big, rough guys asking if the pot of Swiss Raspberry Supreme coffee is ready always makes me smile.

Unlike many northeastern trout streams, which tend to be mildly acidic in their water chemistries, the Battenkill is moderately alkaline. This attribute is derived from the valley's limestone bedrock, which is abundant between Dorset and Arlington. There are numerous marble outcroppings in both Dorset and East Dorset, which gave rise to a major quarrying industry here lasting through all of the nineteenth century and more or less ending with the First World War. During this period almost 16 million cubic feet of marble were extracted from as many as 25 separate quarries in town, some remnants of which are visible from almost any roadside. There are presently no active quarries in Dorset, although its stone was used for many well-known buildings around the United States, including the New York Public Library in Manhattan.

The West Branch Battenkill flows generally parallel to Route 30 between Dorset and Manchester. There are again no fishing-access areas specifically marked as such, but in a few spots the river can be easily reached from the highway. Wild brown and brook trout are both present, the stream is not stocked, and fishing quality will depend on the ease with which a particular spot can be reached. As usual, the more difficult the access, the better the fishing.

The Battenkill's main headwater tributaries come together at Manchester, including both branches from the Dorsets as well as Bourn, Bromley, and Lye brooks that come tumbling down from the high, mountain country east of town. These eastern highlands are part of the Green Mountain Range and lie within the Green Mountain National Forest, which was established in 1932. Its boundaries were recently extended to include the Taconics west to the New York State line, although actual land acquisition in the new portion is just getting underway. The national forest offers numerous opportunities for hiking, camping, and hunting, as well as brook-trout fishing in several high-elevation ponds and small streams. Detailed maps and other information are available from the Forest Service

A portion of the newly refurbished Equinox Hotel at Manchester, VT.

Manchester District ranger station on Route 11/30 east of Manchester proper.

Manchester itself is a well-known tourist town and has been such since the 1850s. Its attractions are too numerous for listing here, but are thoroughly described in the recent book *An Insider's Guide to Southern Vermont* (M. Bucholt, ed., New York: Plume/Penguin, 1991.), to which I was a contributing author. Charles Orvis started the fishing-tackle company that still bears his name here in 1856, three years after his older brother Franklin began the almost as well known and spectacular Equinox Hotel. The grand, old frame hotel has been

Part of Manchester's growing commercial district, now famous for factory-outlet stores.

through various incarnations since 1853, most recently a 1991 refurbishing by Guinness, the British brewer and present owner. Restoration included the complete rebuilding of the hotel's 18-hole golf course. The hotel is the centerpiece of a Manchester Village historic district that includes numerous nineteenth-century homes fronting a tree-lined street with marble sidewalks; the American Museum of Fly Fishing; a white-painted, gold-domed county courthouse; and a quintessential New England Congregational church with a high steeple and wide doors that open on the village green. It's a popular scene that's become a New England cliche, one created perhaps most strongly here in the homespun mythology of Vermont where white clapboards and maple leaves are in some way the stock in trade of every successful business.

There's a different world just down the street. In addition to more traditional activities of golf, fishing, skiing, tennis, or just relaxing, Manchester has become a mecca for outlet shoppers. There are approximately 150 retail businesses in town and roughly a third of these are newly arrived factory outlets with trendy names such as Ralph Lauren, Calvin Klein, Brooks Brothers, and Esprit. People who once came to put their feet up are now pounding the sidewalks, loaded with shopping bags and looking like a weird caravan somehow lost en route between New York and Montreal. The influx of shoppers has been a substantial benefit to locally owned businesses, including a small antiques shop run by my wife and myself. Even so, the retail-growth question has become the most politically divisive issue in recent local memory, and town officials are struggling to find ways to ensure diversity and orderly development in what not long ago was a one-horse downtown district.

Manchester's resident population of approximately 3,500 swells to 20,000 or more during holiday periods, when traffic at the town's one central intersection may back up for a mile or more. Perhaps most important for a potential visitor is knowing when *not* to visit Manchester, at least if one wishes to avoid the throngs. Crowds are greatest between Christmas and New Year's Day, during the Presidents' Week holiday period in February, Fourth of July weekend, Labor Day weekend, and are at their maximum during the first two weeks of October, which is typically our peak season for fall foliage.

Among the area's many scenic attractions, fishing the Battenkill was widely promoted by tourist-hungry railroads after the Civil War, as well as by Manchester's assorted innkeepers and by Charles Orvis and the subsequent owners of that rapidly growing tackle business. That promotion has continued more or less unabated for almost 150 years, although railroads dropped from the picture after World War II, with the result that the river's national reputation as a trout stream far exceeds the actual fishing. There are more and larger trout to be had in many Rocky Mountain rivers by virtue of their greater size and productivity, as well as in certain northeastern waters, such as New York's Beaverkill or Connecticut's Housatonic, by virtue of their enlightened management as catch-and-release waters in the face of heavy angling pressure. To its credit, New York manages four miles of its lower Battenkill under severely restrictive creel limits with correspondingly improved fishing. Vermont, which like its towns along the river is so adverse to change, continues to apply the state-wide daily creel limit of twelve trout to the Battenkill as it has since 1957 when the limit was reduced from twenty trout daily. For the state's most intensively fished wild-trout stream, this anachronism produces trout of ever decreasing size for ever increasing numbers of fishermen. So be forewarned. It's a lovely stream that's now more rich with angling tradition than with trout. The fishing is almost invariably pleasant, if not especially productive. Most of your catches will be less than ten inches long, and you'll often be working very hard to obtain even a few of these. Locally experienced anglers of some skill sometimes score better, of course, having learned times, fishing spots, and unmarked access points that often aren't available to visiting fishermen.

There's some lovely meadow water along Manchester's Battenkill, notably on Oscar Johnson's farm from the Richville Road bridge back upstream toward town. This area is unposted private land, the continued availability of which depends on the manners of visiting anglers, so keep it clean. Downstream of the same bridge is a long, brushy river reach controlled by the Perkins family, present owners of the Orvis Company. Access to this area has traditionally been by limited numbers of free day permits, available at Orvis's Manchester store on Route 7-A. While technically unable to regulate fishing on the river *per se* because it's a public waterway subject to regulation by

Part of an Ogden Pleissner retrospective I assembled for The American Museum of Fly Fishing after his death in 1986. *Photo courtesy American Museum of Fly Fishing (AMFF)*.

the state, the family to their credit has long made catch-and-release fly fishing a condition of access over their adjoining land. One long-term result is brook trout that are both larger and more numerous here than anywhere else on the river. Another, less-fortunate result has been the response of some local anglers downstream who, having at least partly depleted the downstream public river sections, have plenty of snide things to say about supposed elitism upstream. Such attitudes are as short-sighted as they are inevitable, and harken back to the first Neanderthals who fought over a piece of meat.

Sportsmen who speak of Manchester and the Battenkill almost always speak of Ogden Pleissner, the late landscape artist, in the same breath. Pleissner lived near Manchester's Bourn Brook above the Battenkill from the time of his second marriage in 1977 until his

death in 1983. He had earlier moved from New York City to nearby
Pawlet, Vermont, in 1947 after touring western Europe as a war-time
illustrator for *Life* magazine. He was quite successful as a landscape
artist and after the war was rarely forced into more mundane illustration work. His upland hunting and fly-fishing scenes — those for
which he's best known locally — were a minor portion of his work and
also artistically the least successful. But his fishing paintings such as
the 1971 *Lye Brook Pool* and *The Battenkill at Benedict's Crossing* in
1978, both of which were issued as limited-edition prints, quickly became icons among Battenkill anglers, perhaps because no artist of
equal or greater prominence has painted the river so well.

The Hill Farm stretch at Sunderland town is the next prominent
river feature as one travels downstream from Manchester. Here the
river meanders through low, open meadows, and here you'll find a
state historic marker along Route 7-A marking the former home of
Ira Allen, Ethan's brother, who was also active in the state's eighteenth-century settlement. The adjacent town highway bridge over the
river offers access to the Hill Farm, where very large brown trout are
occasionally taken and brook trout are sometimes abundant. The
trick in fishing here is to sneak within casting range of rising trout by
crawling on one's hands and knees through the grass. Walking upright along the bank or wading in the river itself almost invariably
spooks those trout you're trying to catch.

Arlington is the next town downstream, also on Route 7-A, and
here the Battenkill makes an abrupt westward turn, flowing for about
seven miles in a narrow water gap through the Taconics and into New
York. The river is closely paralleled by Route 313, making for easy access, and is more open and wide in this stretch, averaging seventy-five
to one hundred feet from bank to bank. It is the most popular area
among anglers, and fishing pressure here measured in terms of anglers
hours per season is as much as four times that received by other popular Vermont trout streams such as the New Haven or White rivers
farther north. This area has also become increasingly popular for
canoeists and inner-tube floaters on summer days, and there's now so
much river traffic that midday fishing is impossible. As the number of
floaters escalates annually, conflicts with riparian landowners are also
increasing. The problem is rapidly getting out of control, has become
politically contentious, and there's no local solution in sight.

The best way to see what Vermont's Battenkill Valley looked like fifty or more years ago is to travel the lower river in New York. Here the landscape has escaped the gloss of tourism characteristic of the upper valley, and remains primarily agricultural. Morning mists along the river carry the cloying smell of cow manure freshly spread on adjacent fields, and the diesel exhaust you might also smell almost certainly comes from a big, green John Deere tractor rumbling through a cornfield rather than from a newly polished Mercedes sedan. The region is refreshing in its reality and lack of pretension, and I often travel downstream to fish here for that reason.

There are about eighteen miles of productive trout water along the 'Kill as one travels downstream from the state line toward Greenwich. The first four miles from the state line to the covered bridge at the Eagleville are restricted by New York to artificial lures only with a daily limit of three trout ten inches or longer. This section isn't stocked; its abundant brown trout and less common brook trout are all wild. This is the section favored by many fly fishermen, many of whom travel here on day trips from nearby Albany or Glens Falls, and is crowded on weekends and during periods of major hatches. It also is the continuation of the popular floating section in West Arlington, and flotillas of canoes and inner-tubes have in recent years made midday fishing difficult here as well. Angling access areas with parking along this stretch are numerous and most are clearly labeled as such by the state.

There's one fly shop in this area, which is a good source of local information and trout flies. My old friend George Schlotter has been running the Battenkill Anglers' Nook on Route 313 west of the state line for more than twenty years, and most of the lower-river regulars hang out here at odd times between hatches. I have often thought the best way to learn to fish the 'Kill would be to spend a Saturday here in May or June, listening quietly from a corner. Amid the endless flow of jibes and good-natured insults come priceless snippets of fishing lore, the sum of decades of experience with the river's often difficult trout. George's trout flies are first-rate, usually tied with premium dry-fly hackles from the roosters he raises for that purpose behind the shop. In recent years, he's bred sufficient birds to have dry-fly necks for sale in a variety of natural colors including several shades of dun.

George Schlotter with one of the roosters he breeds especially for flytying at Shushan, NY.

The Battenkill here is the boundary between the towns of Salem on the north and Jackson on the south. The latter includes the district known as Shushan, which is where the late Lee Wulff lived from 1940 until 1960, when he moved to Keene, New Hampshire. These were the years during which Wulff first established his wide reputation as an angler and conservationist, although he wrote about the Battenkill itself relatively little. Wulff and I became friends in his later years through our mutual association with several fishing magazines, and I spent parts of one winter rummaging with his help through sixty years of his old clippings, eventually compiling many of them as *The Compleat Lee Wulff*, published in 1989 (E. P. Dutton; New York). This book contains as much of his Battenkill work as I could find.

A few months before his death in 1991, I spent a day driving with Lee and his wife, Joan, around Shushan and the lower 'Kill. We

Lee Wulff fishing below Shushan's Spring Hole a few months before he died in 1991 at age eighty-six.

George Washington Bethune, editor of the first (1847) American edition of Walton's *Compleat Angler. Photo courtesy AMFF.*

stopped to look and to fish at the Spring Hole, one of the river's best-known pools, located where County Road 61 crosses the river by the old Buffum place. "It hasn't changed much," Wulff told me, smiling and pulling on his waders. "It's still country." We fished enough that cold afternoon to say we'd done it, although none of us caught anything. One of the last images I have of my old friend is that of a tall figure in a downstream riffle, silhouetted against the Battenkill's sparkling flow.

Access to much of the lower river is by Routes 22 and 29, which join near Salem village, a sleepy little crossroads a couple of miles north of the main stream and located on White Creek, a major tributary. This is where George Washington Bethune grew up, attending the Washington Academy here until 1819 when he left at age 14 to attend New York's Columbia College. He eventually became a well-traveled minister in the Dutch Reformed Church, serving parishes in Rhinebeck, NY, Philadelphia, and in Manhattan, but is important to anglers as the editor of the first American edition of Walton's *Angler*, published in 1847. Bethune appended copious notes on American angling to his Walton edition, which still offers what's probably the most complete account of American fly-fishing practice before the Civil War. He acquired his taste for angling during his Salem boyhood years along White Creek and the Battenkill under the guidance of a character known in local histories only as Fisher Billy. Bethune's fishing teacher was by all accounts a bum, hiding out in rural Salem from his creditors at Albany and elsewhere, but within his teaching and within the Battenkill itself were the roots of one of American angling history's most important works.

There have been a great many others, of course, and I'll stick my neck out here to say that the Battenkill—directly or indirectly—has been responsible for a greater body of angling writing than any other American trout stream. This is not directly related to the river's fishing, which itself is worth no more than a small book, but is also more than mere happenstance.

Another notable work was John Harrington Keene's *Fly Fishing and Fly Making*, which went through three editions starting in 1887. Keene was British, emigrating to America in 1885 after having grown up in a fishing family and both writing and fishing professionally in England for a number of years.[4] He settled in or near Manchester, Vermont, in 1886, apparently in loose association with Charles Orvis and his then-thriving tackle company. By 1888, the opinionated Keene and even more opinionated Orvis had had some sort of falling out, and Keene moved down the Battenkill to Greenwich. He lived, fished, and earned at least part of his living along the lower Battenkill as a commercial fly tier until about 1900, when he went through a series of moves that included Maryland and southern New York. Keene ultimately died of a cerebral hemorrhage while in residence at the Brattleboro (VT) Retreat in 1907, by which time he was a confirmed alcoholic and had also been diagnosed as having syphilis.

He was a prolific writer, contributing frequently to *The American Angler* and other periodicals, and his angling work was far more advanced than any of his American peers. By the time he arrived along the Battenkill, Keene had already had long experience with British brown trout, which are notorious for being more critical of fly patterns and tactics than the Battenkill's (or any other) brook trout. That he never achieved great popularity among angling readers is almost certainly because the sophistication he offered in tactics and fly patterns — so essential in brown trout fishing — wasn't necessary in brook trout fishing. By the time dry-fly fishing for newly introduced brown trout here became popular after World War I, Keene's work was being eclipsed by that of Theodore Gordon and others in rivers farther south.

The lower Battenkill has cradled other angling writers, too, including *Lee Wulff*, two of whose early works — *Leaping Silver* and *The Atlantic Salmon* (first edition), both based on his experiences with Canadian salmon — were written while he lived along the river at Shushan between 1940 and 1960, together with dozens of magazine pieces in the same period.

The upper river has had a greater share of angling authors and editors, extending back to the 1883 book *Fishing with the Fly*, a collection of angling anecdotes Charles Orvis co-edited with his friend A. Nelson Cheney. This was quickly followed in 1892 by the massive and often-reprinted *Favorite Flies and Their Histories*, compiled and edited by Orvis's daughter, Mary Orvis Marbury. By 1916, the Orvis Company was in decline following the death of both Orvis and his daughter, and remained as such until resurrected by D. Clark Corkran after World War II. There was a parallel hiatus of the Battenkill in print that was broken by the late John (Jack) Atherton of Arlington with his wonderful 1951 book, *The Fly and the Fish*.

In 1972, Don Zahner moved his fledgling *Fly Fisherman* magazine to Dorset, near the Battenkill's headwaters, from St. Louis where he'd earlier been working as a public-relations executive for Seven-Up and had coined the phrase "un-cola." The magazine was on shaky footing then, and as Zahner liked to say, "Dorset is a nicer place to go bankrupt than St. Louis." The magazine prospered, however, and I came on board as an editor in 1975. *Fly Fisherman* was eventually sold in 1979 and was moved to Pennsylvania a few years later. I stayed in the Manchester/Dorset area and started both *Rod & Reel* (now *Fly Rod & Reel*) and *Fly-Tackle Dealer* magazines during the late 1970s and early 1980s. These, too, were eventually sold and moved to Maine in the mid-1980s, although I by choice stayed put with both feet in the Battenkill.

During the same interval, a number of other sporting writers settled along the upper river, and their combined output has been enormous. The late Craig Woods of Dorset, one of my former *Fly Fisherman* associates who died tragically young, found metaphorical treasure along the Battenkill as expressed in his book *The River as Looking Glass*. Many years ago, a kid named Tom Rosenbauer arrived in my publishing office with a rough manuscript about which we talked for a long time. Now he's a senior executive with Orvis in Manchester with four very worthwhile angling books to his credit. Lionel (Tony) Atwill, Robert Jones, and Geoffrey Norman all moved independently to Dorset during this period; are all highly successful writers for a variety of national magazines; and each has written several books while still finding time to fish between deadlines. We occasionally hold informal and unscheduled meetings at the village post office to gripe at each other about picky editors and slow-pay publishers.

For more than a century, artists and authors have found something in the Battenkill Valley conducive to their lines of work. That something is not just the fishing, which is pleasant but not outstanding. It was that question that started me wondering about *why* the Battenkill is what it is, which goes far beyond a simple physical description. Several years ago, my friend Bill Herrick did an *a capella* monologue for a local Trout Unlimited dinner, basing his lines on an old routine by comedian Mel Brooks called "The Two-Thousand Year-Old Man." In this case Herrick was The Two-Thousand Year-Old Angler, wearing cave-man attire and sporting a fly rod when he announced that "Ah, yes. The Battenkill's a great stream. I fished it when it was in Idaho."

As you're about to see, Herrick was close to being right.

CHAPTER 2

The Taconic Problem

*T*he night boat from Albany to New York City was noisily chugging its way down the Hudson River under summer stars, its progress made slower this night by a coming tide and the prevalent southwest wind. A deckhand stood quietly in the bows, occasionally tossing a lead and gaging the depth with long sweeps of his arm as he retrieved the sunken line. The glow of a thousand small lights passed slowly by on the east bank, the night lights of Poughkeepsie held secure by a thousand glass chimneys in perfect parlors. There was no shoal water here, which the deckhand knew from hundreds of such nightly trips. And there was no need to signal the river's depth to the helmsman, who knew the river as well as he knew his boat.

A second figure stood motionless at the railing midships, partly obscured by huge bales of wool that covered the foredeck and to all appearances lost in thought. The man was James Hall, who by this year of 1849 had become internationally famous for his research and publications on the geology and paleontology of New York State. Almost as well known was Hall's long-standing feud with fellow geologist Ebenezer Emmons, one of Hall's instructors at the Rensselaer School during the 1830s who, during the 1840s, had formulated a geologic theory concerning the Taconic Mountains of northeastern New York with which Hall violently disagreed. Hall was messianic in his life-long pursuit of scientific correctness, an attitude that was in large part responsible for his notoriously difficult personality. On this night his mind was as much on sabotage as it was on science.

Hall finally turned and went into his small cabin, returning with an oil lamp with which he found his way below decks. In the jumble of crates and sacks destined for the New York market, he found the long wooden box containing Emmons's newly printed geological charts of New York, which Emmons was shipping from Albany for ultimate distribution throughout the state's public school system and which were partly based on Emmons's theories of the so-called Taconic System. Hall dragged the box up a narrow ladder to the deck and quickly slipped it over the side and into the dark Hudson water. With self-righteous satisfaction, he watched Emmons's work float away from the boat, sinking lower and eventually disappearing. In Hall's view, Emmons was wrong. The integrity of American science must be protected, and Hall was then its self-proclaimed if warped protector.[5]

Hall wasn't alone in his condemnation of Emmons's work, being joined by the eminent Louis Agassiz at Harvard and the widely respected geologist James Dwight Dana at Yale, among others. Emmons's theories were hotly contested in the letters columns of Albany newspapers by Agassiz, Dana, and a handful of other scientists, who also pursued a lawsuit over the same topic that dragged through the courts at Albany until 1851, at which time the suit was declared unreconcilable and therefore a non-suit. In that year, Emmons left New York in scientific disgrace brought on by the weight of contrary opinion, taking a post as state geologist in North Carolina where he died in 1863. His theories fueled some of the most vigorous and long-standing arguments in the history of American science. Eventually, Emmons was proved at least partly correct, but such proofs came only with the emergence of modern theories of plate tectonics in the 1960s. Emmons's arguments had their beginnings — and ultimate end — amid the rocks of the lower Battenkill.

The geology of the Battenkill Valley explains a great deal of both the river's history and its present character. Much of the river's volume, for example, is derived from spring flowages in the surrounding hills, flowages that are themselves the product of a geology that is, in the northeast, at least, unique. Geological processes, of course, are responsible for the shape of the valley and, in turn, the land-use patterns that have been imposed upon it. Questions of the region's geology are also far more than seemingly quaint quarrels among nineteenth-century scientists. For example, during 1992 several hearings were held by a Vermont state environmental board concerning a proposed housing development near an area of several springs that are the source for the Battenkill's West Branch. One question at issue was and is the relative porosity of the underlying bedrock and whether or not — if the rock is indeed porous — effluent from conventional, in-ground septic systems would find its way into the springs. Each side in the contested hearing introduced the testimony of its own consulting geologist, professional scientists who — predictably — disagreed as to whether or not the region was a "karst," which means an area of fractured limestone rock offering numerous passages for underground water. At this writing, the question — and the proposed development — is unresolved.

The arguments posed by Ebenezer Emmons were deceptively simple, and arose when he was given some trilobite fossils found by his friend Asa Fitch during the early 1840s in the hills of Greenwich, New York, overlooking the Battenkill. Emmons concluded that the rock strata in which the trilobites had been found was older geologically than those strata directly underneath, correctly basing his conclusion on the supposed age of such fossils as found elsewhere. Unfortunately, Emmons's conclusion — that part of the Taconics (and thus Battenkill headwaters) was composed of older on top of younger rock — contradicted completely the foundations of what was then modern geology; namely, that younger rock invariably overlies older rock. This had been proven time and again by Agassiz, Dana, and others through their analysis of numerous fossil records elsewhere.

Folded rock in a West Arlington ledge along the Battenkill, reflecting the forces of ancient tectonic collisions.

Emmons's claim was the equivalent of telling the enormously popular Agassiz that his life's work was in error, which accounts for the overwhelmingly violent response of the scientific community to Emmons's ideas.

But Emmons was right, although neither he nor his opponents lived long enough see the question at least partly resolved, and the answer is deceptively simple. Most of the Taconic Range in southwestern Vermont and adjacent New York—including the western side of the Battenkill Valley—is characterized by westward thrust faulting, a geological process though which immense layers of rock are literally shoved on top of others. By rough analogy, shoving a scattering of magazines into a rude stack accomplishes a similar result in which the magazines slide over one another like layers of rock and wind up in a pile that doesn't reflect their original order. The forces behind such thrusting obviously were enormous, and modern geologists now attribute such movements to plate tectonics, which describes continents as floating islands that are carried to and fro by convection currents deep within the earth's molten core. Ancient continental collisions are now seen partly as mountain-building events, responsible for both the Taconic and Green Mountain ranges that overshadow the upper Battenkill on the west and east respectively. Emmons's trilobites, to complete the tale, apparently originated somewhere along what was once our northeastern continental shelf, and the rock containing their fossilized remains was eventually shoved hundreds of miles westward, ultimately overlying obviously younger formations in the Taconics because of a tectonic event.[6]

There are three distinct physiographic regions surrounding the Battenkill, which is not especially unusual for any river that eventually flows through different sorts of country. What is unusual is that the three regions are at once so geologically different and geographically so close together; several different accidents of geology conspire at once to make the Battenkill unique. Looking south from a point of high land in the vicinity of Manchester, Vermont, all three areas are evident at once. On one's left and to the east is the western front of the Green Mountains, an abrupt and dramatic scarp rising as much as 2,000 feet above the valley floor. Directly ahead and running due south parallel to the scarp is part of what geologists call the Vermont Valley, a relatively flat, glacially gouged valley that ranges from less than a mile wide near the East Branch Battenkill origins at East Dorset, Vermont, to as much as eight miles wide near Bennington. The Vermont Valley begins in west-central Vermont near Brandon, and extends some 85 miles south into Massachusetts. Finally, on the immediate right and west are the High Taconics, a second north/south trending range dominated by 3,816-foot Mount Equinox at Manchester, Vermont.

Before exploring each area further, here's one brief example of the diversity of their influences on the river itself. The relative flatness of the Vermont Valley gives the river its slow, meandering character. With only one major exception (the Green River in

The Valley of Vermont, looking south from a Dorset mountaintop toward Manchester. The Green Mountains are at left, High Taconics at right.

Sandgate and Arlington, Vermont, which enters from the west), all of its major, surface-water tributaries enter the upper Battenkill from the east and are tumbling, nutrient-poor mountain streams that cascade out of the Green Mountains into the valley. In sharp contrast, the tributary flows entering from the west are derived almost exclusively from springs surfacing either in the High Taconics or along the western edge of the valley floor.

Surface-water inflows from the east tend to be warmer than the mainstream in summer, tea-stained by the humic matter of high-level swamps, and subject to severe flooding in times of snow melt or heavy rain. Trout fishermen often call such waters freestone streams. Inflows from the west are consistently colder than the mainstream in summer, clear, and of comparatively constant volume over time, characteristics trout fishermen often associate with spring creeks. Most trout rivers are one or the other. But within its unique geology, the Battenkill is the sum of its parts — part freestone stream and part spring creek while being neither one completely.

The Green Mountains are Vermont's principal mountain range, a portion of the Appalachians that extends for about 160 miles through the state in a north-south direction. The range is roughly 30 miles wide as it parallels the upper Battenkill between East Dorset and Arlington, Vermont, and of slightly lower elevation than the high peaks farther north in the same range. Stratton Mountain east of Manchester is the highest local peak at 3,936 feet and generally marks a difference in watersheds. Streams to the west of Stratton are typically westward flowing, eventually into the Battenkill and Hudson drainages, while streams to the east feed systems of the West and Connecticut rivers to the east. The mountains are conspicuously rounded, and glacial scouring plus subsequent erosion has exposed Precambrian gneisses along their summits. This ancient and very hard metamorphic rock is among the oldest known on earth, dating back some one billion[7] years, and approximately 500 million years older than the various schists and other erosion-prone rock that still cover the mountain flanks and that once covered their summits.

Above the steep escarpment that forms the valley's eastern wall, the mountains slope upward more gradually for several miles eastward until the height of land is reached. Within this area are several small high-country ponds and numerous brooks offering brook-trout fishing that ranges from merely good to exceptional, depending mostly on the season. Soils are thin over a granitic base, producing the mildly acidic environment typical of higher elevations in the northeast and generally dictating the area's ecology. Fishermen hiking to these remote waters in early June will thus find both pink lady's slipper (a wild orchid) and showy blooms of red-and-white painted trillium to be relatively abundant amid mixed stands of maple, beech, birch, spruce, and fir, while plants less tolerant

Float-tube fishing for brook trout in remote Bourn Pond, Green Mountain National Forest. *Photo by Jason Merwin.*

of soil acids — such as oak trees and white trillium — are generally absent.

The high-altitude ponds themselves — Beebe, Branch, Bourn, and others — are typical of northern ponds that are slowly evolving into acid bogs. Pitcher plant, sundew, bog rosemary, and other plants characteristic of acid bogs are found at least to a limited degree around the shores of all of these ponds, while occurring nowhere else — to my knowledge, at least — in the Battenkill drainage. Remote Bourn Pond is the most advanced in this natural aging process and has the greatest abundance of floating vegetative mats and accompanying bog plants. These ponds together with numerous high-elevation beaver bogs and flowages all have dark tea-colored water that results from tannic acids and other humic material leaching from vast accumulations of decaying plant matter. The color persists in tributary streams flowing from the ponds and high-level swamps, which is why the Battenkill's water, while quite clear, is also the color of very weak tea. This is one of many reasons why the river's brown trout are so difficult to catch; because the water is of the same hue as the fish themselves, often the trout are hard to spot.

The Battenkill's Green Mountain tributaries have cut steep, narrow-walled ravines through the mountains' western wall. Stream

The Roaring Branch in high water.

gradients here are severe, ranging from 150 to as much as 800 feet of vertical drop per mile of stream. Their creek beds are often characterized by large boulders, some as large as a car, that move violently in times of high water. The aptly named Roaring Branch, which joins the Battenkill at Arlington, is the largest of these and the most easily accessible, paralleled by the Kelley Stand Road (closed in winter) that leads into the mountains from East Arlington. It's a lovely spot in summer as the creek gurgles around huge rocks in the shade of towering hemlocks; a welcome refuge for picnickers, fishermen, and swimmers. In spring snow-melt or after heavy rains, the creek's upper reaches are terrifying; great masses of water descend like a runaway freight train, rolling tons of boulders and filling the narrow ravine with a loud roaring noise. I have felt the streambank vibrating under my feet at such times, and heard the clicking, grinding bumps of the moving rocks even above the water's roar. Having satisfied my curiosity — and been frightened — I've returned only at gentler seasons.

The large, tan boulders common to this and other steep, east-side creeks are primarily quartzite, which is a hard, metamorphosed sandstone. It's a brittle rock, tending to shatter into smaller pieces rather than simply breaking in two when struck severely. The tumbling of such rocks in flood eventually produces smaller and smaller particles of ever-increasing smoothness, and much of the clean, tan gravel so common in the Battenkill's riverbed originates in these violent mountain creeks. The rocks are ultimately sorted in diminishing size as current velocities decrease with altitude. The fine gravels of the Battenkill itself are a function of its gentle gradient along the valley floor, often as little as eight feet of vertical drop per mile of river. This is as much as a hundred-fold decrease from the most severe of its tributaries with a corollary drop in the maximum size of stones able to be transported by the river's gentle current.

What geologists call the Vermont Valley is much more than the simple mountain valley it first appears, being a distinct geological feature in its own right. Often no more than a couple of miles wide, the valley provides a distinct separation in both geology and topography between the ancient gneisses of the Green Mountains on the east and the slates, shales, and schists of the High Taconics on the immediate west. In contrast to both, the Vermont Valley is thickly underlain by limestone and dolostone, which are primarily composed of calcium carbonate and calcium magnesium carbonate respectively. Marble, which is the metamorphic product of both of these minerals, is abundantly bedded in the valley floor and formed the basis for a major quarrying industry that began with what was apparently North America's first marble quarry opened at Dorset near the Battenkill's west branch in 1785.

The calcareous rock is apparently the remnant of billions upon billions of small organisms living in a warm, shallow sea that covered most of the region before a tectonic collision known as the Taconian Event first began thrusting and folding both the Green Mountains and the Taconics some 430 million years ago. The marble beds, especially those at lower elevations, are relatively flat and not folded. Geologists have cited this to mean that these beds remained more or less in place as the Taconics, derived from deeper coastal sediments farther east on what was then the continental shelf, were shoved and folded west over both the newly forming Green Mountains and the ancient seabed of the Vermont Valley. Marble has been quarried here at elevations ranging from 800 feet at the valley floor to as high as 2,000 feet in the easternmost Taconics of Dorset overlooking the Battenkill's east branch and U. S. Route 7-A. I've never seen any reference as to the ultimate thickness of these marble beds, but it appears that in some areas they may be at least a half-mile thick and possibly much more.

These extensive limestone deposits exert a strong influence on the local ecology, including that of the Battenkill. Unlike almost all other northeastern trout streams, which tend to be very mildly acidic, the Battenkill is moderately alkaline, which is a chemical effect partly produced by the limestone of its headwaters. The most expedient measurement is in terms of pH, a scale of relative acidity and alkalinity ranging from 1.0 to 14.0 in which pH 7.0 is neutral, values less than 7.0 are increasingly acidic, and values greater than 7.0 are increasingly alkaline. It's important to know the scale is logarithmic, which means that pH 5.0 is ten times more acidic than pH 6.0, and that pH 4.0 is 100 times more acidic than pH 6.0, for example. The pH of the upper Battenkill, meaning that portion of the main stem in Vermont, averages around 8.0. In contrast, the pH of the high ponds

Rural post office; Rupert, VT., on the headwaters of White Creek, which feeds the Battenkill from the Taconic west slope.

and Battenkill tributaries rising in the western Green Mountains is substantially lower absent any limestone geology. The logarithmic nature of the pH scale gives the appearance of minimizing what's actually an important difference in water chemistries between the east and west sides of the valley. While parts of this discussion may seem arcane, the principles involved are enormously important in both the region's ecology and in its future.

Limestone bedrock in the valley and western hills contributes dissolved carbonates to both surface and ground waters feeding the Battenkill. Rain and snow interact chemically with atmospheric carbon dioxide to form a very mild carbonic acid, which makes precipitation naturally and mildly acidic. Limestone is very soluble in this mildly acidic water, with calcium carbonate ($CaCO_3$) dissolving from the rocks as rainwater leaches over and through calcareous bedrock and soils. As these carbonates enter solution they chemically neutralize naturally present acids and gradually raise the water's pH, in this case making it slightly alkaline. If there is no calcareous bedrock, as in the Green Mountain sources of the Battenkill's eastern tributaries, then naturally acidic rainfall remains mildly acidic as surface or spring water, picking up additional acidity from large amounts of decaying vegetation and creating a soil and water environment that is mildly acid in nature. This latter is typical of most northeastern environments in New York and New England as well those of higher altitudes elsewhere such as trout streams in the high country of Colorado.

Actual concentrations of dissolved carbonates give a more dramatic indication of the differences involved than simply noting slight variations in pH of a point or two. For example, the West Branch Battenkill, which originates primarily as mildly alkaline spring seeps at various locations in Dorset, has dissolved carbonate concentrations ranging from as high as 200 to as low as 115 milligrams $CaCO_3$ per liter of water, depending on the season. In a wet spring, for example, increased surface-water flows dilute carbonate-rich flows from underground. In contrast, the East Branch just a few miles distant contains the discharge of various Green Mountain tributaries and shows dissolved carbonate concentrations that are approximately half those of its sister stream. Even more dramatic differences are shown at higher altitudes in the Greens, with outflows at remote Bourn Pond, which eventually reach the Battenkill through Bourn Brook, showing pH values as low as 5.38 and carbonate concentrations as low as 0.23 milligrams per liter.[8]

These chemical differences manifest themselves in a variety of ways, some of which are still puzzling. The Taconic soils are both slightly thicker and less acidic than those of the Green Mountains, which means oak trees are much more abundant on the west side of the upper Battenkill. Acorns are important forage for white-tailed deer and wild turkeys, both of which are likewise more abundant on the western slopes. Other plants show similar differences in local distribution, such as the high-country wildflowers previously mentioned, and such differences extend to the Battenkill itself. Mosses, rooted aquatic plants, and algae are fairly abundant in the mainstream and western tributaries where currents are slow enough to permit their growth, but are either absent or present to a much lesser extent in the low-carbonate, eastern tributaries.

Trout fishermen have been conditioned by the angling press to view mildly alkaline, carbonate streams as superlative trout waters, which many—but not all—such streams happen to be. The well-known productivity of English chalk streams, such as the Itchen and Test, is partly based on their high alkalinities, as is the fabled fishing of Pennsylvania's limestone country, notably the Letort, Falling Spring, Big Spring, and other calcareous spring creeks in the general vicinity of Harrisburg. Unfortunately, a direct connection between alkalinity and a stream's ability to produce large numbers of wild trout has never been formally demonstrated.[9] The Letort, for example, presently shows dissolved carbonate concentrations of around 100 parts per million $CaCO_3$ in its spring-fed flows with a trout productivity of about 150 pounds per surface acre of stream. In comparison to most streams, its trout productivity is enormous. The Battenkill, with dissolved $CaCO_3$ concentrations ranging from 60 to 200 parts per million is even more alkaline than the fabled Letort but is *substantially* less productive of trout, at present yielding as little as 20 to 30 pounds per surface acre. This is a relatively low figure for a stream of the Battenkill's size and excellent water quality. The puzzle, then, is why the Battenkill doesn't produce more trout, given its apparently exceptional water chemistry. Clearly, alkalinity alone does not magically produce great trout fishing. Other factors are at work, as we'll see in the following chapter.

Relative carbonate concentrations have another ecological effect that extends far beyond variations in the mix and relative abundance of various animal and plant species. Mildly alkaline waters such as the Battenkill are said to be "well-buffered," which means their natural alkalinity can continue to mitigate and neutralize the effects of incoming acids as those acid levels increase. Over the past fifteen years, the increasing acidity of rain (and snow) has gained considerable notoriety as an insidious, invisible pollutant blamed for many things ranging from peeling paint on cars to dying trees to the extinction of fish life in more than two hundred Adirondack ponds. Most — but not all — of the Battenkill system has sufficient inherent alkalinity to be relatively immune from acid-precipitation effects — such as declining carbonates, a falling pH, and a reduction in numbers and diversity of plants, animals, and fishes — at least for the foreseeable future. Certain areas, however, such as the Green Mountain high country with its mildly acid streams, beaver bogs, and ponds, have no such buffering capacity and this lack of carbonate chemistry coupled with their relatively high altitudes places them in *severe* jeopardy from increasingly acid precipitation.[10]

The Taconic Mountains are the third ecologically distinct area making up the Battenkill headwaters, a mountain range with numerous peaks ranging above 2,000 feet that extends north and south along the southwestern Vermont-New York border. These are the hills of scientific controversy that sent nineteenth-century geologist Ebenezer Emmons to North Carolina in disgrace for his ultimately correct interpretation of its rounded masses of seemingly anomalous rock. Most mountain ranges have roots, meaning underlying rocks similar in nature to the mountains themselves. But the Taconics are geologically rootless, a scientific puzzle only recently resolved and one that also has a great deal to do with the Battenkill's ecology in both Vermont and New York.

The tectonic collisions mentioned in this chapter literally shoved portions of a prehistoric continental shelf westward, folding and raising the Green Mountains while at the same time thrusting what became the Taconics over the Green Mountains and to the west. As the Green Mountains continued to be pushed upward, the Taconics apparently slumped farther westward to their present position. The easily cleaved metamorphic rock of the Taconics (slates, shales, and schists) originally covered the Greens, the Vermont Valley, and the Taconics themselves, but were gradually worn away from most of the region during millions of years of erosion. The leading edge of this westward, thrust-faulted rock remains in the Taconics, however, as what geologists call the Taconic *klippe*, a geologically isolated mass of

Manchester-village church spire against 3,816-foot Mt. Equinox, highest of the Taconics.

rock that's truly enormous: some 165 miles long (north to south), ten to twenty miles wide (east to west) and several thousand feet thick according to geologist Bradford Van Diver.[11] Under the klippe are numerous beds of carbonate rock to which the mountains themselves bear no resemblance, hence the anomaly that's only recently been explained in terms of plate tectonics.

Portions of this range adjacent to the Battenkill serve as important recharge areas for underground water as rainwater and melting snow trickle down through hundreds of feet of thrusted, fractured rock, eventually to emerge as springs on both the eastern and western Taconic slopes or in the adjacent valley floors. The region's average annual air temperature is about 47 degrees, and underground water sources almost universally reflect this figure. This is why the Battenkill and its west-slope (Taconic) tributaries remain so cold in summer—almost never exceeding 70 degrees—when other streams dependent solely on surface water become much warmer and correspondingly less hospitable to trout.

From the junction of its initial tributaries at Manchester, the Battenkill flows generally due south within the Vermont Valley and parallel to the mountain ranges on either side. Geologists refer to this pattern as that of a subsequent stream, meaning one that flows parallel to adjacent mountains and which is typical of most rivers. But the Battenkill leaves the Vermont Valley at Arlington, turning abruptly west and running through the Taconics toward the Hudson as a geologically superimposed stream, meaning one that runs at right angles to the trending direction of a mountain range. This is also something of a puzzle at first glance, but according to several geology texts I consulted, modern superimposed streams follow ancient river courses that apparently predate in geologic time the mountains through which they flow. Mountains were thrust upward during the same millennia that ancient rivers were simultaneously eroding downward, with a superimposed watercourse being the modern result.[12]

The Battenkill's abrupt course change was probably also influenced by glacial activity, which gouged the Vermont and adjacent valleys at various periods extending from as recently as 10,000 years ago back some three million additional years. The Battenkill's narrow water gap through the Taconics was likely at one time the outlet of a large lake produced by intervals in the glaciers' ebb and flow, which outlet may have been several hundred feet higher than the river's present elevation. Further, and by the present configuration of adjacent terrain, if the Battenkill were to continue due south, it would have to flow uphill. Large glacial deposits of gravel and other mater-

Exceptional example of Greek-revival style home, a pre-Civil War style most common to the lower valley. This home is in Greenwich, NY.

ials produce a slight upward slope in the Vermont Valley floor immediately south of Arlington.

The Battenkill Gap — as its westward cut has never been called but probably should be — is quite narrow, for the most part much less than a mile wide, but sufficiently river worn over time to be flat bottomed and now mostly meadows within which the river maintains a slow, meandering course. The river is paralleled here by Route 313 through West Arlington and into the New York towns of Salem and Jackson. The water gap from Arlington to Salem is about ten miles long, after which the river enters a region of low, rolling hills — properly called the Low Taconics — extending westward toward the Hudson. The river meanders around the hill bottoms and maintains its slow, low-gradient flow until reaching Greenwich, New York, in the vicinity of which are several low falls over broken ledges.

Finally, and immediately before its junction with the Hudson, the Battenkill's geology has a surprise ending. After flowing for almost fifty miles with a gentle, meandering gradient, the Battenkill drops seventy-five vertical feet over a dramatic waterfall into an equally dramatic gorge extending several hundred yards downstream. Subsequently the river flows for another quiet mile or so, braiding its way into the Hudson through a low, swampy margin. The falls still carry their ancient Iroquoian name — "Dionondahowa" — of which I've seen numerous spelling variants, and can be reached from Windy Hill Road off Route 29 between Greenwich and Easton, New York. In a 1906 state historical publication, E. M. Ruttenber described the name as "a compound descriptive of the locality of the creek, the reference being to the conical hills on the south side of the stream near the Hudson…The sense is 'where a hill interposes…'."

The falls mark the river's transition from the Low Taconics to the Hudson Lowlands, a region of relatively weak Ordovician shales into which the Battenkill cuts deeply and abruptly. The falls also have enormous ecological significance, of which very few people are aware, because they are an impassible barrier to anadromous (or any other) fish. The Battenkill, as well as the entire Hudson River system, never in its history had the vast runs of Atlantic salmon common to other northeastern rivers. Most people, including many fishermen, blithely assume that all such rivers had their salmon runs, which were all more or less extinguished by damming and pollution early in the

Dionondahowa, or the great falls of the Battenkill near the Hudson River. The structure at top diverts much of the flow for power generation.

nineteenth century. But adequate habitat for salmon spawning in the Hudson was never accessible to the fish in the first place, primarily because of tributaries blocked by waterfalls such as those of the lower Battenkill. While the Hudson system does support runs of anadromous fish—notably striped bass and shad—it holds only those sea-run fish capable of spawning in the open waters of major rivers and not those such as salmon that require clean gravel for nest-building in shallow-running tributaries. While historic salmon fisheries were heavily used by native peoples and later white settlers farther east along the upper Connecticut River and elsewhere, which influenced subsequent settlement patterns, the Battenkill had no such bounty. As with so many other questions about the river, the answers are found first among its rocks.

CHAPTER 3

Some Natural History

*A*long the upper Battenkill, there are Dorset ladies with cheeks of tan. They come back in the spring — May, usually — as gaily colored in their country-club cotton prints as the warblers that arrive at about the same time. The warblers have wintered in Central or South America; the ladies in Palm Beach or perhaps Sarasota. You can find the bright little birds if you look carefully along the marshy bottoms where the Battenkill slips darkly without a sound through the alders, and you can hear their sweetly insistent songs in the high Taconic thickets above the village. The ladies are more evident, flocking as they do to the post office, village store, or any of a number of golf courses, much like a Helen Hoskinson cartoon from the old *New Yorker* days: "Oh, darling! How was your winter?" in a voice gone to gravel with gin and pushed past a jutting jaw. These are summer folk, of which, like warblers, we have a great many.

On a recent holiday weekend, one of those in July that brings throngs of hikers, bikers, picnickers, walkers, and assorted other tourists to the upper valley, a veteran Dorset Lady stood outside the post office complaining at length about the traffic. She ended her tirade with a devout wish that her little village could be as peaceful as it was a hundred years ago. At that point, a local man who happens to be well versed in local history stopped reading his mail, turned, and said loudly, "A hundred years ago, you would have hated it here!"

Her eyebrows shot skyward at this temerity from an unknown quarter. I pretended to be reading my own mail and listened through my open car window as the man explained to his reluctant audience that a century ago our little town had been a major center of marble quarries with dust, dirt, and assorted rough characters everywhere. The local population had been much greater then, the man continued, and various forms of commerce more evident; so wasn't it nice that things had settled down so quietly?

The woman had no answer, turned abruptly, and escaped to her car. My neighbor went back to his mail. I drove south down the river valley, smiling at my newfound perspective and braking often to avoid flocks of bicyclists. Many miles downstream and into New York, I finally found a river section free of swimmers and canoes where I sat on the bank, fly rod in hand, hoping to spot a rising trout. Here a yellow warbler flashed brightly above the slow-moving river, snatching a small mayfly from the air and returning to the dark bushes along the opposite bank. The bird's brilliant yellow reminded me of my morning village encounter and set me to wondering what the valley must have been like; not a mere century ago, but before white settlement. The brook trout must have been giants then, measured in pounds instead of scant modern inches, and I might have heard a howling wolf rather than the automobile horn of an irate motorist.

It's a common daydream, I suppose, especially among sportsmen who wistfully long for the days of virgin forests and abundant fish and game. In the Battenkill's case, it's a daydream subject to a pair of common misconceptions. While confronting what's often described as a virgin landscape, the region's first white settlers were in fact coming to a region where native peoples had been active for thousands of years. The relationship between the Indians who periodically used the Battenkill Valley and their environment wasn't always benign. It was,

Dick Finlay setting out for brook trout on Branch Pond, Green Mountain National Forest.

for example, common practice for northeastern Indians of mixed-hardwood forest regions to selectively burn large tracts, clearing by fire the brushy forest understory and making it temporarily easier to see and stalk game animals.[13] The renewed growth following such fires was also beneficial to many woodland-animal species. In recent

years, controlled burns have become an effective — and controversial
— technique in the scientific management of wildlife populations, a
method sometimes now used in the Green Mountain National Forest
headwaters of the Battenkill.

Modern residents of the valley also tend to a parochial view of
their own history, assuming that what took place at one location was
typical of what was happening everywhere else in the region at the
same time. Vermonters are especially prone to such narrow views,
and date the Battenkill's settlement to the 1770s when those who
settled on the upper river first streamed north from Connecticut after
the French and Indian wars. But the Dutch were active in the lower
Battenkill region for more than a century before Ethan Allen, that
most famous of all Vermonters, was born in Connecticut in 1738, and
their impact was substantial.

The best account I've been able to find of what the Battenkill region was like at the time of initial white settlement was written by
Johannes Megapolensis, a Dutch minister, in 1644.[14] By that date,
Dutch settlement of the Hudson region around what's now Albany,
New York, had been underway for more than thirty years, and trade
with both Mohawk and Mahican tribes on the west and east sides respectively of the Hudson was well established. In reading his description, keep in mind that he's describing the country west of Albany,
some thirty miles south of the Battenkill's Hudson River junction,
although I believe most of his words would have applied equally well
to the lower Battenkill itself.

> The country is very mountainous, partly soil, partly rocks, and with
> elevations so exceeding high that they almost appear to touch the
> clouds. Thereon grow the finest fir trees the eye ever saw. There are
> also in this country oaks, alders, beeches, elms, willows, etc. In the
> forests, and here and there along the waterside, and on the islands,
> there grows an abundance of chestnuts, plums, hazel nuts, large
> walnuts of several sorts, and of as good a taste as in the Netherlands,
> but they have a somewhat harder shell. The ground on the hills is
> covered with bushes of billberries or blueberries; the ground in the flat
> land near the rivers is covered with strawberries, which grow here so
> plentifully in the fields, that one can lie down and eat them.
> Grapevines also grow here naturally in great abundance along the
> roads, paths, and creeks, and wherever you may turn you find them....

Lush, summertime growth of ostrich fern makes bankside travel difficult along the lower river.

In the forests is great plenty of deer, which in autumn and early winter are as fat as any Holland cow can be. I have had them with fat more than two fingers thick on the ribs, so that they were nothing else than clear fat, and could hardly be eaten. There are also many turkeys, as large as in Holland, but in some years less than others. The year before I came here [meaning 1641], there were so many turkeys and deer that they came to feed by the houses and hog pens, and were taken by the Indians in such numbers that a deer was sold to the Dutch for a loaf of bread, or a knife, or even for a tobacco pipe; but now one commonly has to give for a good deer six or seven guilders. In the forests here there are also many partridges, heath-hens, and [passenger] pigeons that fly together in thousands, and sometimes ten, twenty, thirty and even forty and fifty are killed at one shot. We have here, too, a great number of all kinds of fowl, swans, geese, ducks, widgeons, teal, brant, which sport upon the river in thousands in the spring of the year, and again in the autumn fly away in flocks, so that in the morning and evening any one may stand ready with his gun before his house and shoot them as they fly past. I have also eaten here several times of elks[15], which were very fat and tasted much like venison; and besides these profitable beasts we have also in this country lions [eastern mountain lion], bears, wolves, foxes, and particularly very many snakes, which are large and as long as eight, ten, and twelve feet. Among others, there is a sort of snake, which we call rattlesnake, for a certain object which it has back upon its tail, two or three finger's breadth long, and has ten or twelve joints, and with this it makes a noise like the crickets. Its color is variegated much like our large brindled bulls. These snakes have very sharp teeth in their mouth, and dare to bite at dogs; they make way for neither man nor beast, but fall on and bite them, and their bite is very poisonous, and commonly even deadly too....

Megapolensis also supplied an account of contemporary fishing, which accounts are extremely rare throughout inland North America before about 1780. His description of seventeenth-century fishing in the upper Hudson is among the earliest I've encountered:

In this river is a great plenty of all kinds of fish—pike, eels, perch, lampreys, suckers, cat fish, sun fish, shad, bass, etc. In the spring, in May, the perch are so plenty, that one man with a hook and line will catch in one hour as many as ten or twelve can eat. My boys have caught in an hour fifty, each a foot long. They have three hooks on the instrument with which they fish, and draw up frequently two or three perch at once. There is also in the river a great plenty of sturgeon, which we Christians do not like, but the Indians eat them greedily.

Many of these fish, of course, were never found in the Battenkill above its great falls near the Hudson, which prevented access by anadromous fish such as shad and eels. Then, as now, the Battenkill above the falls was too cold to support warmwater fishes such as pike and bass. What the Battenkill did have in abundance was brook trout, which the Hudson near Dutch Fort Orange (now Albany) in 1644 was too warm to support. But such was not always the case.

There was a small ice shelf at the edge of the brook, partly covering this merest of trickles a few dozen yards below its mountain-spring source. I tapped the ice with a booted toe to watch its crystal shards tumble in the sunlit current. As the ice flowed away, I was astonished to see a small fish hovering in the water over golden stones where the depth was perhaps two inches and the stream less than a foot wide. It was a little brook trout, all of three inches long, that darted back under the remaining ice when I bent to look more closely.

Somehow, this wiggly bit of a trout was surviving in a stream often so small as to barely cover its back. Even now I find the fish's durability hard to believe. I have watched immense brook trout rising to mayflies in the Labrador moonlight; great hippos of trout that sent ripples far over the surface of the lake and that gave me lifetime bragging rights when I finally caught one or two. But I have never seen a brookie as impressive as that little fish discovered during a winter walk along a Battenkill tributary. Its image in my mind is persistent, much like the fish itself.

Brook trout are abundant in the Battenkill drainage wherever water temperatures remain generally below seventy degrees in the warm summer months. I've found them as far downstream as East Greenwich, New York, although the fish are less common here than upstream as summer water temperatures trend upward as one progresses downstream through New York and toward the Hudson. The merest rivulet or swamp trickle high in the Greens or Taconics will usually hold brook trout as long as its flow is year round and it stays cold, and I've often found small trout in streams no wider than a shoebox where they are sometimes the only fish present. Some larger tributaries, such as White Creek near Salem, New York, are exceptional brook-trout waters by virtue of their cold, spring-fed flows.

An average-size Battenkill brown trout.

Others, such as Black Creek in the same town, are generally too warm to support many trout.

The Battenkill itself is vintage brook-trout water and is today perhaps the largest river south of Maine with a self-sustaining brook-trout population. This is unusual because water temperatures tend to increase with river size, and rivers of the Battenkill's volume are typically too warm for these fish. Larger streams thus often support only brown or rainbow trout, both of which are more temperature tolerant than brookies. It is the river's numerous springs, both those originating in the Taconics and those in the riverbed itself, that keep almost all of the Vermont 'Kill below seventy degrees even in August, an influence that extends for several river miles into New York. In the same late-summer interval, many other northeastern rivers,

A large spring high in the Taconics at Dorset, one of many such feeding the Battenkill.

including some other well-known Vermont trout streams, may occasionally reach as much as eighty degrees. For brook trout, such
temperatures are lethal.

The brookie's specific scientific name is *fontinalis,* which loosely
translated from Latin means "living in springs." It was so named in
1758 by Swedish naturalist Carrolus Linneaus in his book, *Systema
Naturae,* which formally established binomial, latinized nomenclature
in the natural sciences. Linnaeus included brook trout in the genus
Salvelinus, which he apparently derived from an ancient Scandinavian
word for charr. Brook trout are more closely related to other
members of the charr group, such as lake trout and Arctic charr, than
to "true" trouts of the genus *Salmo,* which includes brown trout.
Brook trout were first called "trout" by Europeans new to North

America who saw the fish's superficial resemblance to the native brown trout of Europe, and the name has persisted in usage. The taxonomic reference to living in springs refers to the brook trout's cold-water requirements; brookies (and most other fish) can't live in springs *per se* because water emanating from underground is usually so oxygen-poor as to limit their survival. After spring flowages tumble, mix, and become aerated over a surface distance of several yards from their outflow, the water becomes oxygen rich while remaining cold and often ideal for trout.

The brook trout's prehistoric ancestors were cold-water marine forms that colonized inland waters with the ebb and flow of glacial activity as recently as 12,000 years ago. As the ice sheets went through cycles of advances and retreats, trout habitats were created, persisted for a few millennia, and then were eradicated by climatic change and the again advancing ice. The brook trout's modern distribution was a result, and its endemic range extends from far northeastern Canada west to Michigan and northern Iowa and south along the Appalachian spine as far as Georgia. This distribution generally follows a gradient of compatible water temperatures, which means that brookies are found only at increasingly higher elevations in southern parts of their range. Brook trout may have originally entered what came to be the Battenkill system via the Hudson at a time when glacial melting meant the Hudson was both colder than at present and at a substantially higher level. Or the fish may have come via the Champlain Sea, a large inland sea of which Lake Champlain is a modern remnant. In that case the fish would have tended south and into the Valley of Vermont, populating both Otter Creek and the more southern Battenkill in the process.

It surprises many people, most especially non-anglers, to learn that brook trout are the only troutlike fish native to the Battenkill system. The brown trout so common here at present were first imported to North America from Germany in 1883, and the Battenkill itself apparently received no brown-trout introductions before about 1920. Rainbow trout, which were formerly stocked in the Battenkill but never established themselves as a naturally reproducing population, were originally indigenous only to the Pacific Coast, and their range wasn't expanded eastward until the American trout-hatchery movement began in the 1870s.

Brook-trout fishing in Bromley Brook, Manchester — a worm-fisher's version of heaven.

Brook trout, then, first colonized and then evolved within the Battenkill system for several thousand years before the ecological disruption caused by white settlement. While these cold-blooded fish lack the publicly appealing, soft, brown eyes of a deer or the cuteness of a rabbit, brook trout are *the* native species most synonymous with the river itself. As such they are both vastly important and — unfortunately — grossly neglected in both public attitude and in modern management.[16]

To provide some comparison with what happened to the Battenkill's brook trout from the eighteenth century onward as described in following chapters, here's some of my own educated guesswork as to what the river and its trout were like in the year 1644 when Johannes Megapolensis was writing his description of the nearby upper Hudson.

First, the Battenkill was slightly colder in summer than at present. No land had been cleared, so the river and its tributaries were shaded to a greater extent. Even though beaver were abundant in the high, flat swamps around what became Manchester, Vermont, the warming effect had by their ponds on the river's flow was more than offset by shade and numerous springs. This means that brook trout were found much farther downstream than at present, probably at least intermittently all the way down to the great falls near the Hudson. Second, the river's flow volume was probably somewhat less than it is now. Because the entire region was forested, more surface and ground water was lost through evapotranspiration, the process by which tree leaves yield water to the atmosphere, thereby affecting the flow volume of adjacent rivers.

The river was slow-flowing and meandering then, as now, and its edges were littered with fallen trees and woody debris to a vastly greater extent than at present. These partial obstacles to the river's current were (and are) quite literally trout hotels, forcing the current to dig deep, shaded pockets under log jams that were ideal hiding places for trout. Such overhead cover has been shown in modern studies to limit some trout populations by its absence, and this trout cover on the 'Kill has been in steadily diminishing supply for more than two centuries since land clearing began in the late 1700s.

The brook trout themselves were both larger and more numerous, although not as large as many fishermen might suppose. As one

Shadbush in blossom — May on the West Branch.

progresses northward in the brook trout's range from Georgia to Labrador, the fish tend to become increasingly large and longer-lived. The extreme and rare cases are those brook trout of far northern Labrador and Quebec, which in certain waters may reach twelve to sixteen pounds weight and a maximum age of twelve years. These old giants, most commonly of eight-to ten-pounds weight, are invariably found in very large and remote river and lake systems that are for the most part unobstructed by dams and subject to very little pressure from anglers. Their longevity has been described as a survival adaptation for severe and uncertain northern climates; because old individuals have spawned in each of several years, the likelihood of at least one successful spawning is greatest. This also means that the overall trout population is comprised of individuals of widely varied ages, which minimizes that population's vulnerability to a year or two of bad spawning conditions or some other temporary lack of reproductive success.

In distinct contrast, modern Battenkill brookies almost never live beyond three years old nor grow to a size beyond ten or twelve inches. The largest I've seen in the past fifteen years in the main stream was a measured fourteen inches, and the largest brookie I've heard of locally in recent years was a nineteen-incher of perhaps three pounds that was caught in a tributary's swamp flowage. For the past two hundred years, fisherman have been catching and removing the river's largest brook trout, removing from the trouts' genetic pool those attributes of size and longevity. The fish are smaller now, partly as a result of the foregoing, and shorter lived, which means the present day brook-trout population is vulnerable to one or two poor spawning years such as might be caused by drought or flooding.

Brook trout of the extreme south are generally small and short lived. The opposite is true in the far north, and the Battenkill of three-hundred years ago unquestionably came somewhere in the middle. The fishing here in 1644 — that fishing about which I daydream so often — would have been outstanding for brook trout ranging up to six pounds, but averaging two to three pounds at lengths of sixteen to nineteen inches. The largest fish might have been six or seven years old, with most fish living through their fifth year and spawning in each of at least three consecutive years. In the little high-mountain tributaries, a ten-incher in 1644 would have been a giant, just as now. These little streams are and were generally such infertile, hostile environments between spring flooding and summer drought as to make their production of many larger fish impossible.

It had rained during the night; a warm April rain that dripped in cheerful, tinny *plinks* on some old tin buckets under my back-shed eaves. The buckets have been there for a long time. I could move them, of course, but won't because I like the rain sounds. I set out to go fishing that morning as the sky cleared, an idea just as quickly abandoned when I stopped near the river and saw how the Battenkill had risen, spreading over the water meadows at Sunderland like a glistening quilt with patchwork reflections of sky and clouds.

Early May blossoms of hepatica in a High Taconic woodland.

There would be no fishing because of the high water. I felt lost for a moment. After a long winter, the day was, as the late cartoonist H. T. Webster once observed, "…too hot for long underwear and too cold to go swimmin'." I finally decided to walk down along the river anyway, taking some boots to get through the large puddles, along with some small jars and a butterfly net with which to catch a few of any mayflies that might be hatching in spite of the high flow.

The river was starting to drop a little, although the riverbank was still a few inches underwater in spots, and I finally reached the river's edge after picking my way around the deepest areas in the flooded meadow. A few large mayflies floated here and there on the surface, and I eventually spotted one that I could catch as it rested on a meadow-grass tuft a few inches above the flow. As I walked over and started to reach with my net, the insect disappeared in a gray blur of movement.

A small bird had swooped down, snatching the mayfly within inches of my grasp. It was a myrtle warbler, one of many warblers that seem to arrive each spring in the valley at about the same time as the first aquatic-insect hatches in late April. As I watched, the little bird darted from a still-leafless alder thicket to snatch another fly along the bank. We played a brief game, the bird and I, along the bank, which the bird invariably won, reaching any mayflies that I might have caught long before I could get within range.

These are the birds that I most closely associate with the Battenkill and with trout fishing. The river's low, brushy banks are ideal habitat for many warbler species from its Vermont headwaters all the way to the Hudson. During the early season, meaning late April through May, I might encounter ten or more different species somewhere along the river. Some, such as the locally rare Tennessee Warbler, are transients, filtering through the valley for a week or two in spring while heading for breeding areas farther north. Yellow warblers, yellowthroats, black-and-white warblers, and others remain all summer, but are most easily seen in spring before dispersing to local nesting sites. The flashes of brilliant yellow commonly encountered by fishermen, hikers, and canoeists along the river's banks are usually yellow warblers; other species tend to be more secretive and take a little more looking. The best way to see the river's varied bird life is by canoe in early May, traveling the river silently at a time when

Pink lady's-slipper — Green Mountain National Forest.

spring foliage is not fully emerged and the newly arrived birds are less hidden by the leaves.

There are other birds along the river, of course, and the most casual observer will sometimes see blue herons, assorted flycatchers, numerous cedar waxwings, mergansers, various common ducks, an occasional osprey, and — rarely — a bald eagle that's come up the valley from the Hudson or is otherwise in transit. On summer days there will be a variety of hawks soaring high over the river bottoms, with red-tailed hawks seemingly most common. Near any one of many large, flat marshy areas you might also hear a sound that puzzled me for years until I took the trouble to investigate its source. While fishing the Sunderland meadow water in spring I had often heard a faint, high winnowing sound of no readily apparent origin. I finally noticed a small bird flying so high as to be almost invisible against the blue sky, and watched the bird plummet suddenly to earth, disappearing near a marshy cattail clump. It was a common snipe in courtship ritual, and the sound is made by the bird's rapidly moving wings in high-altitude display. You'll see or hear other snipe-like birds as well, from the nasal *peent* of a woodcock in thickets of a May evening to the quick movements of spotted sandpipers among the riverbank stones to the insistently shrill whistles of killdeer in the summer meadows, each found according to its own preferences in a remarkably diverse valley habitat.

Such habitat differences are primarily a function of the region's geology and topography as explored in the previous chapter, and are unusual in that their variety occurs within what's really a small region. This extends to a variety of botannicals as well as to birds, mammals, and fish, and the Vermont Valley is well known among amateur botanists for the presence of certain calcium-loving plants that aren't found in the adjacent and mildly acid Green Mountains, for example. When Miss Frances Theodora Parsons[17] first published her book *How to Know the Ferns* at Albany in 1899, she noted that a Mrs. E. H. Terry had found thirty-three fern species plus four varieties during a two-hour walk around the Battenkill headwaters at Dorset. This is a remarkable number within such a short range and is again indicative of the region's habitat diversity. I will also confess to considerable amusement at the image of these intrepid amateur botanists of the Victorian era carrying a lunch packed at the village inn and setting forth in hot competition for the greatest number of species in the least possible time. My own interest in collecting the region's aquatic insects is probably seen with equal humor in some quarters and will doubtless be seen by my own grandchildren as being equally quaint.

Pitcher plant, a juglike plant common to acid bogs, at Bourn Pond, Green Mountain National Forest.

There are surprises in the high country, too, and at this writing it's possible to hear coyotes yelping in the hills while listening from the edge of an open fairway at the local country club. These moonlit howls sound the same in New York and Vermont as they do in Montana, but seem somehow out of place here. Eastern coyotes have become increasingly common in this area since the 1940s and are now well established. These are not domestic-dog hybrids—or "coydogs" —as once commonly believed, but pure-strain coyotes that are much larger than their western relations. The average body weight of mature males here is around thirty-five pounds[18], and those few that I've seen in the wild have been more heavily furred and shaggier looking than those I've seen in the Rocky Mountain states. From my home high in the Taconics, I hear their howls most commonly at night in January and February and sometimes on spring afternoons when young-of-the-year coyotes seem to first find their voices. It's a glorious and eery sound and one that I still find difficult to associate with moonlight in Vermont.

When hiking or fishing the national-forest high country along the Battenkill's eastern tributaries, it's increasingly likely that you'll encounter moose. If you're not familiar with moose, this can be a real shock. Mature males will weigh from more than 600 to almost 1,200 pounds, are more than six feet tall at the shoulders, and carry antlers

Wild turkeys in winter — Dorset's High Taconics.

in season that will look twenty feet wide if met on a narrow woodland trail. Moose populations in northern New England and New York have been increasing dramatically over the past several decades, and their range has been extending southward as a result. There are now breeding populations in the Green Mountain high country east of the upper Battenkill valley where, until recently, the animals had been extinct since the early nineteenth century.

In speaking with some federal wildlife biologists, I was surprised to find that the introduction of timber wolves to this region had been recently contemplated and then rejected. Wolves elsewhere are the primary predator of moose, with Alaska and Lake Superior's Isle Royale being the best-known examples of this interaction. Wolves, of course, were once native to the Battenkill region, but were eliminated early, as soon as 1800 or shortly thereafter. Any thoughts of their reintroduction were abandoned because eastern coyotes—with which wolves would in some ways have to compete—had become so well established.

There are other large carnivores in our hills, notably black bear and bobcat, both of which are secretive and rarely seen by casual hikers. In many years of wandering the woods, I've seen a bobcat only once, which was a couple of years ago high on Mother Myrick Mountain above the Battenkill's west branch. Both fisher, a large member of the weasel family, and pine martens have been successfully reintroduced in the high country east of the 'Kill, and the reintroduction of wild turkeys in the 1970s has been spectacularly successful. These immense woodland birds are now numerous, and the raucous gobbling of a big tom is a sound often heard by evening fishermen where the river runs near the mountain slopes.

And maybe—just maybe—there are lions. Whether or not there are any eastern mountain lions in the mountains surrounding the Battenkill—or anywhere else in the northeastern U. S.—is the subject of considerable interest and dispute. Rare sighting reports from reliable individuals over the past several decades—including some from the Green Mountain high country—have fueled the argument, but no one yet has produced photographs. Regional wildlife officials acknowledge the possibility, but attribute such rare sightings to animals escaped somehow from captivity. Since mountain lions aren't your average household pets, and because security at formal zoos is quite strict, I find this explanation lacking.

Vermont's last mountain lion—maybe. This 182-pound cat was shot at Barnard in 1881. *Photo courtesy AMFF.*

At one time, of course, mountain lions, or catamounts as they're sometimes known locally, did roam the Battenkill region. The last specimen known from Vermont is thought to be a 182-pound cat shot at Barnard, about fifty miles north and east of the Battenkill, in 1881. The lions' historical prey was primarily whitetailed deer, populations of which had been drastically reduced by 1800, mostly because of overhunting. The extensive land clearing that began late in the eighteenth century also diminished the lion's habitat, and the lions themselves were subject to a bounty starting in 1779 that wasn't repealed until 1904. At present, the eastern mountain lion is listed by Vermont as an endangered species, which is tacit acknowledgment that it might exist.

There are other animals of note, a few of which are covered briefly in later chapters, and foremost among these are beaver. In my own fisherman's view, beaver are a nuisance. In recent years they have proliferated, the result of reintroductions in the 1930s after the animals' extinction around 1800, and their dams can be found within roadside view of almost every regional highway and secondary road. While such dams and ponds often create temporarily good brook-trout fishing, they also slow and warm the tributary flows and thus affect the thermal ecology of the entire river. There are now so many beaver in the Battenkill drainage that the animals are no longer simply content with the damming of suitable tributaries and have moved into the mainstream itself. Many of the Battenkill's long, still pools in both Vermont and New York are now home to bank beaver in areas where the river's size precludes their dams. The animals are relatively unmolested, and many of those in the mainstream have become accustomed to human activity nearby. My evening fishing in many such pools is now often interrupted by beaver swimming in front of me and slapping their tails on the water, either in alarm or as a territorial imperative. I'm not sure which. In any case, their splashing frightens the trout I'm trying to catch, and I've often been forced to move to another pool while hoping that beaver will be absent.

I am fond of wildlife in general, but the Battenkill's beaver are rapidly becoming too much of a good thing. Beaver (and other) trapping appears to be a declining activity in the Battenkill region, perhaps because their pelts have faded from fashion and thus decreased in value. Then, too, the decline of trapping is probably generational. The few older men in the area who once trapped all started trapping as kids; country boys these days seem more concerned with video games than with trap lines, for which I can hardly blame them. Trapping is a cold, messy business. Beaver are big animals, commonly weighing forty pounds and even more, and other than trappers have at present no significant predators. They are fun to see and to watch at times, but they are proliferating in the Battenkill region with few natural controls and soon may be seen more widely as a real problem.

CHAPTER 4

Indians and Allens

*M*any histories of the Battenkill region are most re-markable for their misconceptions. For example, my 1978 edition of the *Vermont Atlas and Gazetteer* (Freeport, ME: DeLorme Publ. Co.) includes the following historical note, which is grossly incorrect:

> Prior to the coming of the Whiteman [sic], the present state of Vermont was largely an uninhabited no-man's-land. The entire area was a disputed hunting ground claimed by the Algonquin tribes of indians, who resided in what now is Canada, and the powerful Iroquois federation, whose principal villages were in what is now New York state.

This simply isn't true, as we'll see shortly, but exemplifies the kind of thinking found in most local, regional, and state histories that

begin their accounts with eighteenth-century white settlement and ignore more than 8,000 years of Native American activity in this region
altogether. Such attitudes evolved logically enough, since newly
arrived white settlers after 1750 apparently found the upper valley
empty of human activity and assumed such had always been the case.
Only in the past two or three decades has sufficient — and still sparse
— archaeological evidence emerged to paint a very different picture.[19]

This scholastic misdemeanor has become compounded by melo-
drama, which has continued more or less unabated since Samuel de
Champlain took a few potshots at some Iroquois Indians while exploring northwestern Vermont in 1609. The entire region from Massachusetts
north and well into Canada eventually became embroiled in a long
series of intermittent colonial wars involving the British on the south,
the French to the north, and, to a much lesser extent, the Dutch on the
west along the Hudson, each with their respective Indian allies. Regional hostilities finally ended with the 1763 Treaty of Paris, in which
French Canada was formally ceded to Great Britain. Accounts of this
era are uniformly long on Indian atrocities and short on the Indians'
rapidly dwindling civilization. Crisfield Johnson included this typical
version in his 1878 *History of Washington County, New York*:

> The French records show nearly twenty such expeditions in that year
> 1746 that went on their mission of murder to the frontiers of New York
> and Massachusetts. Most of them passed over some part of the
> long-extended borders of Washington County, but it would be idle to
> recount the meager annals of these inglorious exploits, so much alike
> in their atrocity and in their insignificance save to the unhappy victims.
> One week a band of painted warriors (perchance led by one of their
> own chiefs, perchance by a French officer almost as wild and fierce as
> themselves) would be gliding swiftly through the primeval forests on
> the banks of Wood Creek, the Hudson, or the Batten Kill toward the
> doomed locality; the next week the same forests would shadow their
> returning forms as they hastened toward Canada, their dark faces
> gleaming with triumph, their girdles adorned with the scalps of old and
> young, male and female, while in their midst there would perhaps be a
> few haggard men and weary women, urged forward by their brutal
> captors, and shuddering at the unknown fate which awaited them.

Shades of Hawkeye! James Fenimore Cooper's fictional hero
would have undoubtedly ranged along the lower Battenkill in New

York during the French and Indian wars, given the times and places described in Cooper's 1826 novel, *The Last of the Mohicans*. The Battenkill Valley in Vermont and New York was, in historical fact, part of the Mahican (the presently accepted spelling of Mohican) homeland, which extended roughly from the height of the Green Mountains in southwestern Vermont westward to the Hudson and slightly beyond.[20] Unfortunately, fictional accounts such as Cooper's and historical accounts such as Crisfield's have become almost indistinguishable, and the common perception of the region's native peoples has become that of a short and bloody frontier romance leading to the equally romantic American revolution. Yes, it was sometimes bloody; and yes, there were some extraordinary acts of heroism. But there was also much more.

The first people in the Battenkill region were almost certainly what are now called Paleoindians; small, nomadic groups of hunters following caribou and other large game northward as the last great ice sheets retreated more than 10,000 years ago. As archaeologists William Haviland and Marjory Power report in their excellent 1981 book, *The Original Vermonters*, Paleoindian artifacts found in southeastern New York (about 100 miles due south of the Battenkill) have been radiocarbon dated to approximately 10,500 B.C. Similar materials — including fluted, stone projectile points and stone scrapers used in processing meat and hides — found in Nova Scotia have been dated to 8,600 B.C., which together with other data lead Haviland and Power to suggest that Paleoindians were drifting into Vermont almost 9,500 years ago. Among the limited number of sites at which such materials have been found regionally, most are along the immediate west side of the Hudson River trending chronologically south to north or in the area of Lake Champlain, both of which waterways were substantially higher than their present levels because of glacial melting. It may have been that the Battenkill Valley, being relatively narrow, was so flooded as to be avoided by wandering hunters. If not, the narrowness of the valley might have concentrated herds of migrating caribou and other game, in which case it could have held a temporary Paleoindian camp that was periodically reoccupied during annual game-animal migrations through the region. This is speculation, of course, and to my knowledge Paleoindian

Congregational church on the green, Manchester Village — viewed through columns of Equinox Hotel.

artifacts have never been rigorously searched for nor found in the immediate Battenkill vicinity.

Around 7,500 B.C., the thin spruce forests of our tundralike landscape gradually changed, becoming dominated by pine and oak as part of an ongoing global warming. The big-game animals hunted by Paleoindians eventually disappeared from the region, as apparently did the natives themselves, their way of life no longer matching the region's changing ecology. The regional archaeological record appears generally blank until about 6,000 B.C., which is the approximate earliest date of artifacts from the so-called Archaic Period. This era lasted until about 2,000 B.C., and is characterized in part by the development of an increasing variety of tools, including those made of slate with ground edges and adaptable to a wide variety of cutting and scraping tasks. Evidence of Archaic human activity in the Battenkill Valley is, again, largely circumstantial, but quantities of late Archaic artifacts have been found along the Walloomsac River some thirty miles south, near Bennington, as well as along Otter Creek north of Rutland. Interestingly, a copper gorge, which is a primitive style of fish hook, was among those artifacts uncovered at one Otter Creek site. This device could easily have been used to catch Otter Creek's brook trout and could just as easily have been used to catch the more abundant Battenkill brook trout a few miles south. Both Otter Creek and the Battenkill flow partly through the long Valley of Vermont, and human movement between the two would have been easy. Thus we have our first Battenkill fishermen possibly dated some 2,000 years ago, a conclusion achieved only by inference.

The Woodland Period followed the Archaic, although certainly not as an abrupt transition. According to Haviland and Power, our northeastern climate had stabilized, more or less, to its modern form by about 2,300 B.C., and forests in the region were as they are now, at least in general terms of the species mix. Smaller projectile points emerged early in this period, indicating the development of bows and arrows that could be used to hunt newly abundant species such as moose. The gathering of woodland plants, fruits, and nuts had become an important adjunct to hunting; dugout canoes (and eventually those of birchbark) were in use; and by about 500 A.D. agriculture was becoming increasingly common. The Woodland Period extended to the first contacts between various Indian tribes and European explorers, which occurred as soon as the early 1500s in northeastern maritime regions and as late as 1609 with the explorations of Champlain and Hudson. Archaeologists and others refer to these meetings collectively as "contact" and often cite certain events as being either "before contact" or after.

Artifacts from this era have seldom been found along the Battenkill, but are apparently common in valleys to the immediate

Camped at Bourn Pond shelter, Green Mountain National Forest.

north and south. The only formal Battenkill "dig" of which I'm aware took place during the early 1960s in a Shushan, New York, cornfield then belonging to the late Lew Oatman, who at the time was a well-known fisherman and fly tier. This flat riverbend land yielded a number of stone artifacts, including a stone mortar and pestle, that were excavated from below plow depth. That Woodland Indians were using the Battenkill Valley is, I think, beyond argument, and the lack of additional hard evidence is perhaps most attributable to a lack of looking.

European contact was a disaster for native peoples of the Battenkill region and elsewhere in the northeast. Epidemics of small-pox, diphtheria, and other diseases to which natives had no immunity began as early as 1535 in the St. Lawrence Valley and over the next 200 years devastated Indian populations throughout the region. The

Indian population of New England has been estimated at 90,000 individuals before contact, which was then subjected to a disease-related fatality rate of ninety percent! Historian Colin Calloway, based on his extensive study of northeastern native peoples, describes such events even more strongly:

> These lethal pathogens were truly the shock troops of the European invasion of America, and the result was one of the world's greatest biological cataclysms. Reports of scarce Indian populations, in northern New England and across the continent, usually described a situation that existed after epidemic disease had obliterated major concentrations of population.[21]

Here we've come full circle from the common assertion of a historically empty region to the evolution of a native civilization over several millennia that was all but wiped out by two centuries of disease. The Battenkill Valley was apparently never subject to the widely known raids and battles that extended from New York and Massachusetts well into Canada as part of the French-and-Indian and other intermittent colonial wars that finally ended in 1763, being in this interval nothing more than a corridor that was sparsely settled, if at all. Instead of picturing eighteenth-century painted savages, I have in my own mind an image several hundred years older: that of a small band of fur-clad Mahican hunters carrying heavy loads of moose meat down the steep ravine of Arlington's Roaring Branch after a snowy, high-country hunt. The Battenkill Valley is a familiar and easy two-day trip back to their winter camps on the upper Hudson, where the meat will be a welcome meal typically followed at fireside by the old men's tales of times long ago.

They say the grave digger never whistled at his work but once, and that was the day in 1783 when he buried Ethan Allen's first wife, Mary. By local lore, Mary Allen was a first-order termagant. Dorothy Canfield Fisher of Arlington, the late (1879-1958) novelist still regarded as southern Vermont's first lady of letters, included this anecdote in her 1953 book *Vermont Tradition*:

> Ethan Allen had ridden down to Bennington to pass a cheerful evening with tavern cronies. Some of the lively Arlington boys in the horseplay

years of their teens made themselves weirdly tall by draping sheets from broomsticks held up over their heads, and hid behind the marble tombstones. When Ethan came along, these eight-foot-tall white specters ran out to the road, screeching that they were devils come to carry him off to hell.

Ethan Allen waited composedly till his voice could be heard, and said, "Go back to your master Beelzebub, and tell him I said I fear him not, for I married his sister!"

That remark purports to be vintage Ethan. Of the few important historical figures closely associated with the Battenkill Valley, none is more famous than the half-legendary Allen. Within his eighteenth-century life here, and amid events such as the Vermont-New York border conflicts in which he was the central figure, are found many of the reasons why the upper Battenkill Valley in Vermont and the lower river in New York are to this day so radically different. Such differences are most evident in the landscape, with the commercial whirlwind of flashy retail outlets, golf courses, and ski areas near the upper river at Manchester being in dramatic contrast to the gently rolling farmscapes of Salem and Jackson, New York, just a few miles downstream. These contrasts extend far more deeply than landscape, however, and include deeply rooted differences in such things as local-government form and even in the corn-harvesting methods used by local farmers on either side of the state line. There are differences in attitudes, as well, with some Vermonters even now tending to a certain smugness about their state and its history, while some New Yorkers still look upstream with suspicion and resentment. The most consistent thread through all of these differences is Ethan Allen himself.

After about 1960, when waves of second-home development began to spread rapidly across southern Vermont, the term "land speculator from Connecticut" became a dirty phrase, often uttered as a curse by locals who, perhaps rightly, resented the condominiums that were sprouting like manure-pile mushrooms on the mountain flanks. How ironic, then, that Ethan Allen, our regional hero of heroes, was himself a land speculator from Connecticut who traveled Vermont in search of a fast buck—or a fast shilling, to be more historically precise.

My having said this will bring a strong chorus of groans and "Yes, but's…" from many Vermont readers and some equally loud "I told

Bennington Country Court House; on the green, Manchester.

you so's!" from New York. More than two hundred years of popular, highly romanticized history have Allen and his famous Green Mountain Boys variously banishing the savage Indians, wresting control of Vermont from the evil New Yorkers, winning the American Revolution almost single-handedly, and keeping Vermont as a republic independent of the first thirteen states until 1791 because — then, as now — you can't be too careful. As a general case, historians over the past twenty years or so have taken an increasingly revisionist view, in the course of which any number of towering heroes have been revealed as clay-footed clods who happened to get lucky. It's not my intent to debunk the Allen mythology for the mere sake of debunking, and I do believe he was a genuine hero. But later works such as Charles Jellison's exceptional 1969 biography of Allen have made it increasingly clear that Allen was indeed mortal, that he was subject to the same temptations of greed, guile, and excess that confront anyone else, and that he indulged in all three to an extraordinary degree.

By 1740, political boundaries and land ownerships between the Connecticut and Hudson rivers north of Massachusetts proper — including most of what is now Vermont — were in assorted degrees of dispute. In 1674, King Charles II had confirmed an earlier land grant to his brother (and, later, king) James, the Duke of York (and, hence, New York), of lands lying between the Delaware and Connecticut rivers. The colonies of Connecticut and Massachusetts both subsequently succeeded in having their western boundaries established at a line twenty miles west of the Hudson, leaving boundaries to the north unresolved. There was still considerable question as to whether or not the New Hampshire colony extended west to the Hudson or even beyond, or if New York's apparently valid claim of lands east to the Connecticut River was paramount.

It's important to remember that at this time there was considerable pressure for northern expansion from the more settled areas of Connecticut, Massachusetts, and southern New York, where better farmlands were long since taken and small, urban centers were already well developed. Northern land grants became a busy and profitable business. It was common for the original grantees never to set foot in their new "towns" but rather to hire surveyors at a distance and then to sell parcels of often-conflicting title to throngs of eager buyers.

In 1750, Benning Wentworth, governor of the New Hampshire colony, wrote New York Governor George Clinton inquiring as to New York's eastern boundary. While waiting for an answer, Wentworth issued the Bennington land grant, literally establishing a town — on paper, at least — northeast of Albany and almost in Clinton's lap. Predictably, Clinton protested, and Wentworth cheerfully suggested that the British throne to whom they were both obliged arbitrate their case. The French-and-Indian War intervened starting in 1754, but when England finally won control of French Canada with Montreal's fall in 1760, the pressures of settlement and speculation resumed and so did Wentworth. In 1761, he made some sixty major land grants, including all of those towns in what's now the Battenkill region of Vermont. By the summer of 1764, which is when the King found in favor of New York, Wentworth had cranked out a total of 131 grants, all of which sold quickly and increased Wentworth's wealth dramatically. It was, by some views, a colossal theft that was eventually consummated by Ethan Allen.

Allen apparently came to the Grants, as Vermont was then known thanks to Wentworth, for the first time in 1766 or 1767 having been invited by his cousin Remember Baker. Allen and Baker were both originally from northwestern Connecticut, and Baker had settled in Arlington in 1763. After several years of wandering between homes of family and friends in Salisbury, Sheffield, Massachusetts, and near Bennington and along the Battenkill, Allen was finally hired by a variety of Wentworth grantees to represent their interests at the Albany ejectment trials of 1770, which developed as New York authorities sought to assert their control over conflicting land titles. Predictably, the courts at Albany found in favor of disputed New York land titles, and holders of titles evolving from Wentworth grants were advised to settle their claims under New York law.

Allen left the courthouse with his now famous quote, which he may or may not have actually said: "The gods of the hills are not the gods of the valley." Those words, or others to that effect, were a rebellious declaration that soon made Allen and his "Green Mountain Boys" outlaws, at least under New York law. For the next five years, and until the beginnings of the American Revolution diverted attention elsewhere, Allen and his cronies vigorously harassed any so-called "Yorkers" who attempted to settle or otherwise impinge along western fringes of the Grants. Most settlers on the Grants supported Allen at least some of the time, wishing to avoid the tenancy system of nearby New York in which a few wealthy families collected rents from farmers occupying their vast tracts of land. This was a rapidly fading relic of the Dutch patroonship system as represented by families with names such as Schuyler and Rensselaer. But even at those times when New York authorities tended toward compromise, hinting that those Wentworth claims that had been occupied and improved might be honored, Allen persisted. By this time, Allen himself had acquired considerable land on speculation but had neither occupied nor improved any of it himself, which meant that any acquiescence to New York would invalidate his titles.

In July of 1777, town committeemen from among the Grants met at a Dorset tavern on the West Branch of the Battenkill to elect officers for a new Green Mountain Regiment. This was two years after Allen, together with Benedict Arnold, had led the successful raid on Fort Ticonderoga, and Allen was expectant of command. By a vote of 41-5, Allen's friends and neighbors elected Seth Warner as commander, a quiet, strong man by reputation. Nor was Allen among any of the other twenty-three officers elected. As Allen later wrote, "I find myself in favor with the officers of the army and the young Green Mountain Boys. How the old men came to reject me I cannot conceive inasmuch as I saved them from the encroachments of New York."[22]

In relating the incident, I'm reminded of a man in one of our local towns whose demeanor is perhaps similar to that once shown by Allen. This particular fellow is very large and physically imposing, and during local meetings rails on at great length about the virtues of local control and the perceived evils of any state or regional encroachment on individual liberties. He captures an audience by oratorical force, if nothing else, and tends to overwhelm meetings in which he participates. Not long after one such tirade, I ran into a local selectman on the street, a member of the town's elected governing body who often says little. I expressed my concern about the loud goings on, but was assured I needn't worry.

"There's nothing we can do to shut him up," the selectman said quietly, "but we don't always agree with him." And so it was, I think, with Ethan Allen among his peers, who were perfectly willing to have

Vermont's second-highest covered bridge, over the Roaring Branch in Sunderland.

Allen confronting New York on their behalf, occasionally supporting his efforts as needed, but unwilling to invest any elected authority in such an erratic and often pompous man. Although Allen remained politically powerful and often popular, he was most often denied public office.

Vermont was an independent republic from 1777, when a constitution patterned after Pennsylvania's was first adopted, until 1791, when it became the fourteenth state. During most of this interval, various Vermont men, including Allen, badgered Congress incessantly for recognition as an independent entity and eventual statehood. These moves were consistently blocked by such men as the powerful George Clinton, New York's governor, who still sought to assert that state's control over lands to which it had held valid title for more than a century. The republic's *de facto* capitol was at Arlington in the Battenkill Valley, where the stolid Thomas Chittenden had been elected the first governor and where a kitchen-table cabinet composed of Ethan, his brother Ira Allen, Matthew Lyon, and a few others comprising what came to be called the Arlington junto effectively ruled the fledgling state. It was during this interval that what are still the region's most hotly debated events took place; the so-called Haldimand Affair, to which the Battenkill bore silent witness.

Over a period of years, the Allen brothers and others such as Chittenden had accumulated title to large land tracts near what is now Burlington, Vermont, some one hundred miles north of Arlington and fronting on Lake Champlain. Not only was the land potentially valuable as farmland, it also offered easy access to British Canada via the lake and would likely increase in value for its commercial potential. If New York authorities prevailed, in Congress or otherwise, the Allens' valuable titles would be lost.

Sometime in 1780, and well before the Treaty of Paris formally ended the American Revolution in 1783, Allen, in concert with brother Ira, Chittenden, and a handful of others, set out to negotiate an independent truce with British authorities on Vermont's ostensible behalf. I say ostensible because over several months these clandestine contacts evolved into the suggestion that the Vermont Republic should become a quasi-independent colony of the British crown, which would preserve the Allens' land titles in northern Vermont. During the winter of 1780-81, numerous spies were sent by Frederick Haldimand, then British governor general of Canada, some 150 miles south on snowshoes to Allen's home near the Battenkill at Sunderland. There's presently a highway marker near the site, as well as a well-known large spring in the riverbed, which undoubtedly supplied the Allen home with clean and open water in the coldest of weather.

Odd bits of news about the Allens' apparent Tory leanings eventually leaked through the neighborhood and beyond, causing none other than General George Washington to remark that "matters in a certain quarter have a very suspicious face...." Clinton, American General Philip Schuyler, and others assiduously sought proof of treason, but to no avail.

Some — in fact, many — historians have cited the Haldimand negotiations as a sly attempt by Ethan Allen and others to press Vermont's recognition in the American Congress. Others, notably historian Charles Jellison, effectively convict Allen of treason:

> ...it is clear beyond any question that as the negotiations progressed and the pieces of this dangerous transaction began to fall into place, Ethan and his accomplices became firmly committed to the idea of taking Vermont back to the British Empire. By the late spring of 1781, the Arlington conspirators, with Ethan obviously in charge, were headed hell-bent for treason, and that they finally stopped just short of the mark was no fault of their own. 'In the time of General Haldimand's command,' Ethan remarked in a personal letter written several years later, 'if Great Britain could have offered Vermont protection, they would readily have yielded up their independency and become a province of Great Britain.'[23]

The Haldimand Affair ended essentially because of some bungled arrangements that exposed more of the plan than was deemed safe, coupled with the almost simultaneous and distant surrender of Cornwallis and his southern forces to the Americans and French. The revolution was over, and in the subsequent peace treaty of 1783, England effectively ceded to the United States any claims it may have had to the Vermont Republic.

Allen's immediate reputation was sullied, but more by innuendo than any full proof of treachery, which never came to light. In 1784 he sold his Sunderland home, moving with his new wife, Fanny, to Bennington for four years and then ultimately moving north to Burlington, where he died in 1789. Perhaps at least in part because their old enemy was dead, New York authorities finally capitulated, assenting to the admission of Vermont as the fourteenth state in

Eagleville covered bridge — on the Battenkill in Jackson, New York.

1791, at which time Vermont paid New York a paltry $30,000 as resolution of all conflicting land claims between the two states.

Like the native peoples who preceded him in the valley by many centuries, Allen quickly became a romanticized myth, one reinforced by old-timers with selective memories and grasped quickly by newcomers eager to be identified with the rock-hard independence that the Allen myth came to represent. The many half-true legends that now surround his life are partly the result of blanks in the historical record, which have allowed embellishment almost at will. For example, most Allen historians acknowledge that no likeness of any kind apparently survives after Allen's death; there is no contemporary portrait or even a detailed physical description of the man. Whatever you might see in the way of monuments, statues, or paintings are no more than the artists' creations.

I often drive these days out of Vermont and into New York along the Battenkill for trout fishing in the lower river. The state-line passage is like passing through a wall; invisible, but a wall nonetheless. The river valley looks almost the same, but somehow is different. I have stepped from a region that clings fiercely to its town-meeting traditions, and from a region in which county governments are small to nearly nonexistent, into the New York valley where annually elected local supervisory boards serve their towns with no annual meetings, and where county governments are vast by comparison. My neighbors to the rear are distrustful of any authority exerted by their state government, while my friends along the river in front contribute to a huge state bureaucracy from which they expect and demand results.

Ethan Allen isn't responsible for all this, of course, which represents political and social systems that have evolved in slightly different ways over several hundred years. But such differences clearly carry his spirit, or at least what people have ultimately made that spirit to be. I find its best — or worst, as you'll have it — example on the Manchester Village green near the old hotel high above the Battenkill. Here a large statue of a man in revolutionary garb stands mightily on a pedestal, commemorating Vermont's eighteenth-century heros. Ethan Allen? Well, maybe. The statue faces west, toward New York.

CHAPTER 5

A Biological Wasteland

*T*he carefully counting clerks checked and then checked again. It was impossible, but true. Aaron Burr had just tied Thomas Jefferson for the presidency, each man having received seventy-three electoral votes. A week later, on February 17, 1801, and after numerous deadlocks, Jefferson was elected president by the House of Representatives with considerable help from Alexander Hamilton. With that election, a rapidly maturing country entered the new century.

In that same year, and but a few months later, the great wilderness of the Battenkill came to an end. It was cornered against a rock, then shot to death in a drunken rout. It died snarling, but it died. This was the year of the last great wolf hunt in Washington County, New York, when two hundred or more armed men circled a great swamp bent on extermination. Nineteenth-century accounts of that event are both colorful and horrifying. Here's one written during the 1870s in typically melodramatic form:

> ...The farmers and villagers assembled from far and near, armed with rifles, muskets, and fowling pieces, and plentifully provided with ammunition. A captain and necessary subordinates were elected and a list of signals and a code of rules duly promulgated. Then, under the direction of the officers, the circle was carefully formed, and at a preconcerted signal the men advanced into the swamp. Moving forward as rapidly as the tangled undergrowth would permit, they soon began to rouse up some of their victims. Deer sprang from their lairs, and darted away towards the centre of the covert, some falling before the weapons of the hunters, while now and then an old buck would make a bold dash through the circle....
>
> Still onward pressed the hunters, and at length they began to see the gray-backed sheep eaters, the especial object of their search. These, too, retreated towards the centre. The circular skirmish line drew closer. The firing was almost incessant, but it was only at long intervals that a wolf was slain, when shouts of triumph burst from a hundred throats, resembling the scalp-yell which erstwhile rose in these same forests over many a human victim.
>
> Wolves and deer were now intermixed...More and more frequent grew the shots...More and more frequently some of the inclosed [sic] animals dashed through the circle and made their escape; more and more common became the shouts of triumph over the slain. At length the centre is reached amid a grand fusillade of excited sportsmen [!], a frantic scattering of still surviving animals, and a tremendous chorus of yells....[24]

Eleven wolves were shot that day, together with numerous deer and just about anything else that happened to move within that circle of death. I have seen no record of any people having been shot, which is surprising given the large number of guns in close-quarters chaos. Like the surrounding forests, wildlife such as lions and wolves were obstacles to development and were destroyed, while other more providential forms such as deer and turkeys were simply hunted to extinction. Whitetailed deer, for example, were almost entirely eliminated from Vermont by 1800, the victims of over-hunting and rapidly diminishing habitat. By that same year, the human population of Washington County, New York, had reached more than 25,000,

Sheep on a small Manchester farm, a remnant of regional flocks once numbering many thousands.

and University of Vermont geographer Harold Meeks has noted that Vermont's population swelled from 85,000 to 218,000 between 1790 and 1810.[25] This began an expansive era of agriculture and commerce, which for the Battenkill itself was an ecological disaster.

Sheep were the best and the worst of it. The late Dorothy Canfield Fisher of Arlington, that staunchest of all Vermonters in print (who was born in Kansas), gives a long account of Vermont's nineteenth-century sheep boom in her 1953 *Vermont Tradition* while not mentioning sheep in adjacent New York. Crisfield Johnson, the late New York historian, describes nineteenth-century sheep raising in New York's Washington County without mentioning adjacent Vermont. The two lived almost thirty miles and sixty years apart, so this wasn't the result of a direct feud. It's yet another example of the oddly ongoing antipathy along the Battenkill border that makes assembling regional information so difficult.

As of 1807, several important things happened in short order. First, in August of that year Robert's Fulton's side-wheel steamboat *Clermont* made its first round-trip voyage between New York City and Albany, starting a steam-power transportation era that was a vital commercial link between urban markets and those of upstate New York and western Vermont. Farmers along the lower Battenkill could soon trade either south to New York via the Hudson or north to Montreal via Lake Champlain with almost equal facility.

Sometime between 1809 and 1811, depending on which local history one favors, Merino sheep began to be imported to both Washington (NY) and Bennington (VT) counties as well as elsewhere in the northeast. This was a Spanish breed well-known for its abundant, fine wool and substantially more productive than those few rangy sheep previously kept on hillside farms. Wool and textile prices were forced upward by the War of 1812 to levels maintained after the war by the severely protectionist Tariff Act of 1816. Pure-bred Merino rams were commonly selling from $800 to as high as $10,000 apiece, enormous sums at that time, and wool itself quickly reached prices of fifty cents to as much as a dollar a pound. Fortunes were made in both breeding-stock and wool almost overnight. The Battenkill region went sheep-crazy.

It's almost impossible to overstate the impact of the sheep phenomenon; a modern-day nuclear explosion in the valley would have had a similar effect on the landscape. A subsistence farmer raising perhaps a little grain for market in 1805 cleared his land gradually. There was no money to hire cutting crews to rapidly increase his field size. When the same farmer gained sudden wealth in wool, the only obstacle to even greater wealth was trees. Sheep will graze almost any cleared pasture, no matter how steep. Sheep farmers with newly deep pockets were able to clear land at an ever increasing rate because they could hire it done. That meant more sheep. More money. More clearing done even more quickly. By the late 1830s, sheep outnumbered people here by at least five to one. By 1850, almost three-quarters of the *entire state* of Vermont had been cleared of trees, primarily as a result of sheep mania.

While immensely profitable in the short term, this extensive and rapid land clearing was also enormously destructive. Very few contemporary accounts express that view because at the time commerce was far more important than conservation. Among those who did see what was happening was George Perkins Marsh, a well-traveled Vermonter who was born at Woodstock in 1801 and whose now-classic 1864 book, *Man and Nature*, is often cited as the beginning of the American conservation movement. Marsh's description is even now painful:

> With the disappearance of the forest, all is changed. At one season, the earth parts with its warmth by radiation to an open sky — receives, at another, an immoderate heat from the unobstructed rays of the sun. Hence the climate becomes excessive, and the soil is alternately parched by the fervors of summer, and seared by the rigors of winter. Bleak winds sweep unresisted over its surface, drift away the snow that sheltered it from the frost, and dry up its scanty moisture. The precipitation becomes as regular as the temperature; the melting snows and vernal rains, no longer absorbed by a loose and bibulous vegetable mold, rush over the frozen surface, and pour down the valleys seaward, instead of filling a retentive bed of absorbent earth, and storing up a supply of moisture to feed perennial springs...The face of the earth is no longer a sponge, but a dust heap, and the floods which the waters of the sky pour over it hurry swiftly along its slopes, carrying in suspension vast quantities of earthy particles which increase the abrading power and mechanical force of the current, and, augmented by the sand and gravel of falling banks, fill the beds of the streams, divert them into new channels and obstruct their outlets.[26]

The Battenkill quickly became shaded to a lesser degree, growing both warmer and more subject to flooding. Trees that once stabilized the riverbanks were gone, and the river's tendency to cut new meanders in its bottomlands increased, often creating braided channels that divided the flow and further increased the warming effect of sunlight on the water. Instream cover that had sheltered trout and other aquatic species was removed by flooding and not replenished by woody debris from the now-barren riverbanks. These erosional patterns that were so greatly accelerated early in the nineteenth century are to this day persistent along many sections of the river, most notably between Manchester and Shushan in those areas where trees are either noticeably absent or grow at best sparsely along the banks. A modern result is far fewer naturally reproducing trout than the river might otherwise hold if instream cover were more plentiful, together with ongoing problems of erosion in areas where the riverbank has been increasingly unstable for more than 150 years.

The river's early (and recent) problems were not all related to sheep and land-clearing, of course, although these were the most significant. The frantic pace of land clearing and development were bringing about what Charles Johnson in his book *The Nature of Vermont* called a "biological wasteland," which is probably extreme but does dramatize the region's radical changes in landscape. A variety of small mills were being built and operated in the river system as early as the 1760s and in time became extraordinary in number. For example, Hugh Graham, the late historian from Cohoes, NY, once documented thirteen separate mills in nineteenth-century operation on the little Green River in Sandgate and Arlington, most of which were sawmills that dumped prodigious amounts of sawdust and other mill waste into the stream. That pattern was repeated on other tributaries as well, with the Roaring Branch at Sunderland in 1868 boasting eleven mills or factories employing upwards of forty people. There were numerous mills of various types at Manchester and Dorset, including several marble mills, and the development process was repeated all the way downstream to the Hudson. At one time or another, for example, the lower river at Easton, NY, has held saw mills, grist mills, plaster mills, sash and blind factories, cotton mills, woolen mills, fulling mills, flax mills, underwear mills, shirt and dress factories, a tea-tray works, a toy factory, leatherboard mills, a shoe-shank factory, a plow factory, a linen thread mill, various paper mills, and in later years numerous electrical generating stations in a wide range of sizes.

Almost no mention is made in any local histories of adverse environmental effects caused by all this activity, yet those effects must have been substantial. The only explicit reference I've found was given by Tyler Resch in his excellent history of Dorset, in which he noted:

> Marble quarrying had a severe impact on the environment and in 1882 First Selectman William D. Ames of East Dorset did something about it. He filed suit in chancery court against Dorset Marble and D. L. Kent companies for blocking and diverting the headwaters of the Battenkill River with large quantities of sand and leftover marble slabs. The blockage interfered with Ames's 76 acres of "rich, fertile productive farmland," he complained. In 1890 the court ordered the companies to remove their walls, stones, sand, pipe, and other debris, and restrained them from obstructing the river in the future.[27]

What is perhaps most remarkable about that anecdote is that it took an eight-year court fight to remedy such an obvious problem.

Brook trout were able to persist through the Battenkill's nineteenth-century development and gradually increasing fishing pressure only in reduced numbers and gradually diminishing average size. Because of the river's generally low gradient and slow flow, mainstream mills were heavily concentrated at those few locations where the river fell steeply enough to provide efficient power. Then, too, the upper river's abundant streambed springs offered enough upwelling water to keep at least some of the river bottom clean enough for spawning at a time when much of the streambed was otherwise covered with rotting sawdust, marble waste, and silt.[28] Unfortunately, during the 1820s that same attribute of low gradient flow was almost the river's complete undoing.

The lower Battenkill region's rapidly expanding economy was boosted substantially by the construction of two canals: the Champlain Canal that connected Lake Champlain with the Hudson River in 1823, and the better-known Erie Canal that formed a link between Albany and the Great Lakes region in 1825. The financial success of these early canals was outstanding; goods could be hauled long dis-

Fishing the pool at Rexleigh Covered Bridge, lower Battenkill, town of Salem.

tances on canal boats for about $12 per ton instead of the $100 per ton charged by wagon freighters.[29] In 1825, New York Governor DeWitt Clinton, flushed with recent enthusiasm for the Erie Canal, proposed making a canal out of the Battenkill. The Vermont Legislature responded quickly, granting articles of incorporation in October of 1825 to the Battenkill Canal Company and authorizing a few businessmen to build a canal from the state line through Arlington, Sunderland, and Manchester "as far as said corporation shall deem it practical." The Battenkill Canal group was granted extraordinary powers of eminent domain and was to be allowed the "alteration or relocation of public roads and structures," according to their state charter.

Plans for turning the Battenkill into a muddy ditch quickly fizzled, and I'm not sure why. It was one of several contemporary schemes to extend navigation eastward into the Green Mountains and eventually to the Connecticut River, none of which ever materialized. It may be that the mountains themselves were ultimately seen as too formidable an obstacle to east-west commerce, or it may be that fledgling railroads developing farther south as early as 1830 were seen as too much of a potential competitive threat. If the canal had been built, its commercial impact on the valley would obviously have been enormous, entirely changing the region's future. It would also have been the end of the Battenkill as a trout stream, but in the whirlwind world of the 1830s, such an end would have been seen as of little significance.

By the 1840s, the tariffs that had sustained domestic wool prices began to be reduced as U.S. President James Polk sought concessions from the British regarding the northern boundary of the Oregon Territory as well as wider support for a developing war with Mexico. The westward expansion that had been greatly facilitated by the 1825 Erie Canal had also made western wool producers increasingly competitive, and wool prices plummeted in a few short years. The boom was over; by 1850 the Battenkill region had begun an economic decline that lasted for more than a century. Within this period, the respective economies of the upper valley in Vermont and the lower valley in New York began to diverge in ways that are still persistent, with developing tourism on the upper river a distinct contrast to ongoing agriculture and commerce along the New York Battenkill.

Many local histories published within the past century or so make a great deal of what could be called The List of Famous Names, each town declaring pridefully its native sons or daughters who went on to fame or fortune elsewhere. But because of the "elsewhere," it's in many ways a dubious declaration. The achievements of Susan B. Anthony in the nineteenth-century women's movement had very little to do with her having spent some childhood years near the Battenkill[30], and Chester Arthur's U. S. presidency wasn't dependent on his having attended school along the lower river at Greenwich, New York. There are, however, two nineteenth-century native sons who became well known in the lower and upper valley, respectively, and who exemplify the still-persistent and often odd differences between the lower and upper river: Asa Fitch in New York, and Charles Orvis in Vermont.

He was by all accounts an odd little man. You might have seen him along the dirt road between Greenwich, New York, and the Battenkill in the 1840s, as he bent to sweep a small net through the roadside grasses. Any greeting would have been pleasant, brief, and disconcerting because of his hat, which had a life of its own. The black, dusty felt was covered with newly collected insect specimens held securely with fine dressmaker's pins. Here the insects writhed, wriggled, buzzed, and finally died before being removed and cataloged at the Bug House, as Asa Fitch's small office was locally known, between Black Creek and the Battenkill.

Fitch was America's first state entomologist, a post he obtained in New York through the state agricultural society in 1854. As such, he was primarily involved in economic entomology, unraveling the complex life histories of such agricultural pests as the wheat fly, and also working on his own general collections, which eventually exceeded two thousand insect species. He was not a fisherman, nor did he pay any special attention to aquatic entomology, although many of the caddis and mayflies so important to the Battenkill's trout (and trout fishermen) did appear incidentally in his collections. In a broader historical sense, Fitch is most important because he was a scientist, a product of the massive growth in American sciences that took place between 1800 and the Civil War.

By 1830, the upper Hudson region—and particularly the Albany area—was emerging as a center of new science, generally paralleling a few similar developments elsewhere such as the 1812 founding of the Philadelphia Academy of Natural Sciences. In that same year, Stephen Van Rensselaer, one of the last great Dutch patroons, paid for the creation of the Rensselaer School at Troy, New York, agreeing with his friend Amos Eaton, the great natural historian, on the need to "qualify teachers for instructing the sons and daughters of farmers and mechanics...in the application of experimental chemistry, philosophy, and natural history to agriculture, domestic economy, the arts, and manufactures."[31] This was a remarkable change from other contemporary academies with their emphasis on classical Latin and Greek, philosophy, grammar, and etiquette, and was the first

Still-open farm country along the lower river where Asa Fitch wandered before the Civil War.

such technical academy in America. It still exists in Troy as Rensselaer Polytechnic Institute.

Eaton had lectured at Troy in 1819, under Van Rensselaer's sponsorship, on the practical relationships between the region's geology and agriculture, which helped that state's legislature in the same year to appropriate funds for state aid to agriculture. New York and Massachusetts were the first states to take that step. So by 1830, science, agriculture, and the state were firmly wedded along the upper Hudson, including the lower Battenkill region. While farming, milling, and quarrying were equally prevalent along the upper river in Vermont, there was no adjacent cultural center such as Albany to extend the influence of either science or the state into everyday life.

In 1826, seventeen-year-old Asa Fitch traveled from his home at Salem on the Battenkill to Troy, where he met Eaton and was immediately captivated by the older man's kindred spirit of inquiry. Shortly thereafter, young Fitch joined Eaton and others on an Academy expedition to Lake Erie via the new Erie Canal; their company included a young scientist named Joseph Henry who would later become internationally known as the first Secretary of the Smithsonian Institution. Their group tour lasted about five weeks, with morning lectures by Eaton on some aspect of geology or botany, and afternoon lectures by a student chosen for the day and assigned a particular topic. Fitch ultimately spent most of two years at the Rensselaer School, taking a degree in 1827.

Fitch then enrolled at the Vermont Academy of Medicine at Castleton, some thirty miles north and east of Salem, from which he obtained a medical degree in 1829. In his excellent study of Fitch published by the New York State Museum, Jeffrey Barnes noted that early-nineteenth-century medical study was at times difficult because the students, needing cadavers for classes on anatomy and dissection, were often suspected — sometimes rightly — of grave-robbing. Barnes further explained that

> In the early nineteenth century, medical colleges found it a perplexing problem to legally obtain human bodies for dissection and demonstration purposes, so illegal procurement was extensive. The bodies were often obtained surreptitiously at night from some country burial ground. After the Champlain Canal was completed in 1823...many

This Salem village home was remodeled into its present Greek-revival form in 1840.

bodies in barrels of brine marked "pork" were shipped by canal boat from Albany and Troy to Whitehall, then by wagon to Castleton. They were consigned to a merchant in Castleton who was also a trustee of the Academy.[32]

In 1830, Fitch made a second trip west, traveling part of the distance with a second Rensselaer School expedition that was again led by his friend Eaton. One of Fitch's students for part of the trip was James Dwight Dana, who later achieved international fame as a Yale University geologist. Fitch eventually returned to Salem and his Battenkill farm at what's still known as Fitch's Point[33] in 1837. Here he farmed, practiced medicine, and pursued a still growing interest in entomology. By 1847, Fitch had given up his medical practice entirely, concentrating instead both on farming and his study of natural history. Fitch's patient, painstaking work in entomology was finally rewarded in 1854, when New York State appropriated $1,000 for an investigation of the state's insects to be administered by the state agricultural society, which in turn appointed Fitch as its entomologist. He held this post under similar appropriations through 1872. By that time, none other than geologist James Hall, whose chicanery regarding the Battenkill's geology I described in a previous chapter, had become head of the New York State Museum, and it was Hall's politicking that apparently deprived Fitch of his post as Hall successfully sought an appointee closer to Albany and more strictly under Hall's control. By the time Asa Fitch died at Salem in 1879, he had achieved widespread fame in the field of economic (agricultural) entomology and was at the same time nearly bankrupt, his devotion to science having been given at the expense of his neglected farm.

One of Fitch's hobbies was local history, and he collaborated extensively with Crisfield Johnson on the massive 1878 *History of Washington County, New York.* The book is unusual for its numerous large engravings showing large and prosperous-looking farms throughout the lower Battenkill region. Here agriculture was apparently well diversified and sufficiently stable to have survived the drop in wool prices that decimated Vermont farmers farther up the valley in the late 1840s. Part of the reason was (and is) that farmland along the lower Battenkill west of the High Taconics is flatter and more productive than most of the hillside farms of Vermont. Transportation links helped as well, and by the 1850s farmers in the lower valley could ship by either canal or rail to a variety of urban markets. And certainly by this time farming in the lower valley was profitably wedded to the scientific community at Albany with the state continuing to serve as an active matchmaker.

Farmers, mechanics, and merchants from the lower Battenkill were among the audience at Albany on August 27, 1856, when the great Louis Agassiz arrived from Harvard University to address a crowd of 5,000 at the dedication of New York's new state natural history museum. Here Agassiz reminded an enthusiastic crowd of the importance of Albany in the sciences, as evidenced by the American Association for the Advancement of Science again holding its annual meeting in that city. In that same year, and along the somehow increasingly distant upper Battenkill in Vermont, a man named Charles Orvis started a fishing-tackle company.

Tourism in Vermont began with the growing popularity of its mineral springs as early as 1798 when George Round built a frame hotel that would accommodate one hundred guests near Clarendon and its springs some twenty-five miles north of Manchester and the Battenkill. By the 1840s, nationally prominent health spas associated with mineral springs were scattered throughout the state from Brattleboro to Burlington. Louise Roomet, writing for the Vermont Historical Society in 1976, put the popularity of such spas in the context of pre-Civil War reform movements:

> Health was one of the issues reformers adopted and the mineral springs should be viewed within a context which included revivalism, temperance, abolitionism, prison reform, education, and women's rights. Hotels reflected these aspects of the movement as well. During the 1840s a number of Vermont establishments included some reference to temperance in their names.[34]

By the time Franklin Orvis, Charles's brother, consolidated his store and the family home into what he called the Equinox House hotel at Manchester in 1853, both Vermont tourism and the idea of rural hotels was well established. In addition to scheduled stagecoach lines, the Western Vermont Railroad had opened its link between Manchester and Rutland in January 1852, and Orvis was obviously hopeful of further rail links to both steam and rail traffic along the nearby Hudson. I point all of this out because most local accounts cite Orvis's entry into the tourist business as happening early and — with no regional context — out of the blue. Orvis's new hotel was, on the contrary, a shrewd, educated, and ultimately successful guess.

Orvis was also well connected far beyond Manchester. Nancy Otis, in her 1961 history of Manchester, notes that Franklin Orvis "spent some years in mercantile pursuits in Wisconsin, Illinois, and New York before beginning his hotel career" and that he also operated hotels at two locations in Florida for the winter trade. Orvis's hotel did (and does) boast some mineral springs; specifically, three springs high on Equinox Mountain that are not especially high in mineral content because they emanate from rocks above the underlying strata of limestone and marble. While Equinox spring water was bottled and sold for a time, it didn't have the wide "medicinal" appeal of foul-smelling sulphurous springs elsewhere. But by the 1850s, the import-ance of such faddish springs was diminishing, and resort hotels such as the Equinox that remained successful did so by offering a wide variety of activities. Here's a Civil War-era description from the *Manchester* (VT) *Journal* of just what that entailed:

> The number of charming children seen daily in front of the Equinox tells plainly enough that parents think it is a real Family Hotel; and for grown-up visitors, a series of amusements have nightly been extemporized in the large parlor. Plays, Dances, Charades, Concerts, Tableaux, Shadow-Pictures, Fancy Dress Balls, all have in their turn cheered the evening hours. Then there have been excursions to the summit of Mount Equinox, to the Cave in [word omitted] Hollow[35], to Deer Knoll, to the Marble Quarries, to Well's Pond and to Downer's Glen. The Angler has had the finest sport in Bourn and Lye Brooks, in the Battenkill, and in the Equinox Trout Ponds; and the Artist and Author have found congenial subjects for pen and pencil. In short, Manchester has established itself as a favorite summer resort; and if it is so successful now, what will it be when times improve?[36]

The Equinox prospered under Franklin Orvis. Manchester and vicinity was not attracting the "best" of New York, Boston, or Philadelphia; such people went by choice to the fashionable spas at nearby Saratoga, or to Newport, Rhode Island, or to Maine, or to New Hampshire's White Mountains where the scenery was (and is) far more spectacular. But there were enough people in the rapidly growing, urban, upper middle class after the Civil War to make the Orvis hotel business viable. While there were some small resort hotels along New York's lower Battenkill at Salem and Greenwich, the scenery of their adjacent low, rolling hills was less appealing than the high drama of Equinox, and the lower-river region never devel-oped the cachet of Manchester and environs, remaining then as now primarily devoted to agriculture and manufacturing.

Charles Frederick Orvis, Franklin's younger brother, was born at Manchester on June 19, 1831. There are no complete biographies of

Charles F. Orvis in about 1905.

either man, but it appears in reviewing what's available that the energetic Franklin effectively carried the freight while the younger Charles fiddled. At various times, Charles Orvis ran a small summer hotel near his brother's operation, worked as a surgeon-dentist (for which Vermont required no certification at the time), was a village trustee, a fireman, a druggist, a postmaster, and perhaps most often tinkered with things mechanical at which he was by all accounts very skilled. As a tinkering fisherman, he was also making his own rods, which became locally popular. Obviously, such rods could be sold to tourists at his brother's hotel, and so he began his fishing-tackle company in 1856.[37]

The tackle business quickly became a going concern with a growing reputation for quality fishing rods and flies that was producing orders by mail as early as 1861 and the start of the Civil War. Its success is probably more attributable to Orvis's marketing skills as a shrewd and highly energetic promoter than to the fishing on the adjacent Battenkill, which had become terrible and was growing worse. The common assumption is that the Battenkill's supposedly wonderful trout fishing nurtured Orvis's growing business, but that assumption is wrong.

By 1819, for example, the New York legislature found it necessary to specifically prohibit the netting of trout in the lower Battenkill, which even at that early date was like locking an empty barn. In addition to the river damage wrought by livestock and manufacturing between 1800 and 1850 was the effect of railways new to the upper river after 1851. This produced an increase in milling activity at numerous sites, and further encouraged the growth of Dorset's marble industry with its attendant milling and water pollution. By the end of the century, the extension of specialized rail spurs into the adjacent Green Mountains made logging a major industry, which means the fishing in east-slope Battenkill tributaries and in the mainstream suffered further. As a result, the Battenkill and its fishing never attracted the hordes of sportsmen that thronged to the Adirondacks and to Maine between 1865 and 1900. Not only was the Battenkill's great trout fishing long gone by this time, there wasn't much else to attract visiting sportsmen, either. Deer hunters went to the Adirondacks simply because there were no deer in Vermont. In 1878, Vermont imported 17 white tailed deer from New York in an attempt to reestablish its herd, but deer were not prevalent again in the state until the 1930s.

The river's fishing was so bad so early that Orvis often promoted fishing in the Equinox trout ponds instead, as in this news item from the June 11, 1861, *Manchester Journal*:

> Last week C. F. Orvis caught in a short time 27 trout from the artificial pond belonging to the Equinox House, three of which weighed over a pound each; and the entire number averaging three-quarters of a pound. They were caught with the fly, and in three instances two were taken at a single cast.

Such fishing in the Battenkill proper no longer existed. There are a few other accounts of 1861 fishing in local newspapers of that year, and in most cases the catching of *only two* brookies from the mainstream was considered newsworthy.

Orvis succeeded with his tackle business more in spite of the Battenkill than because of it. By the end of the century, the bulk of his business was in mail order, with sportsmen buying Orvis rods, reels, and flies because they were first-rate but using that tackle elsewhere. Because he lived until 1915, Orvis is a convenient bridge into the twentieth century and is further considered in the following chapter. That the area's hotel business also prospered through the turn of the century had little to do with sportsmen or fishing the Battenkill and everything to do with the growing popularity of another sport: golf.

Atherton, Orvis, Rockwell, and Wulff

*A*mong the fishing-tackle customers of Charles Orvis at the turn of the century was George Thatcher, an Albany business-man, fisherman, and golfer who was also part of the group that started Manchester's earliest golf course in 1899. A few years later, in 1909, Thatcher had published at Albany a book containing a wide variety of contemporary anecdotes about Manchester life[38], including the following about his friend Orvis:

> Mr. Newcomer [Thatcher] was somewhat noted as an expert trout fisherman, having been brought up to this sport from his earliest youth, and having studied the ways and habits of this particular genera of the finny tribe, besides acquiring great dexterity in the use of the worm, grasshopper, and the casting of flies. Of late years the game of golf had

attracted his attention to the neglect of fishing, which, of course, shocked the Proprietor [C. F. Orvis] almost as much as it would have done old Isaac Walton. The Proprietor had become a stockholder in the Ekwanok Country Club, but for the first year or two after the establishment of the club had failed to visit either house or links. Finally concluding he would like both to see his investment, and to look upon the ancient game of golf, he went down to the club, and the first person he discerned on the links was Mr. Newcomer...The Proprietor, who was in a jocular mood as usual, attached himself as closely and conversationally as possible to Mr. Newcomer, who with brassey [sic] in hand was about to play his second shot. Of course, the result was a foozle, the ball dribbling along for about two feet to the perplexity of the Proprietor, which, however, did not in the least interfere with his own amazing volubility. Again the swishing stroke and again a foozle, when the Proprietor ceased his conversation on other topics long enough to remark,

"Well, it's too bad to spoil a good fisherman to make a damned bad golf player."

Thatcher, at that moment, did not bludgeon Orvis with a golf club, but later admits he considered it seriously. He did say something to Orvis about being unable to concentrate while Orvis was gabbling in his ear, at which point "the Proprietor seemed to take umbrage and left the links in high dudgeon...."

Thatcher's book is important for a couple of reasons. First, his several anecdotes offer a good sense of what Orvis was actually like. The numerous achievements of the Orvis family in American angling history have been widely described for many years, but their personalities have not, perhaps partly because Thatcher's book, a major source, is far outside the normal chain of angling references. I would not have discovered it but for the kind suggestion of Mary Bort, a local historian.

By local lore, Orvis was argumentative and garrulous; known in the early days of automobiles for confronting drivers near his store and giving them a loud dressing down if he felt their speed was excessive. He was "ornery enough to float upstream" by one newspaper account that appeared long after his death. Thatcher's version is more complete:

Now the Proprietor was a man largely misunderstood by many people. Born with the strictest sense of integrity and morality, he resented all injustice whether on the part of private individuals or public men, and imagined to a certain extent that it was his mission to correct all abuses that came under his observation. The philosophical element was entirely lacking in his makeup, hence he broke many a lance, like Don Quixote, in futile charges against the massive defense of wrongs...it is no wonder that the sarcastic wit, [and] sharp, biting tongue of the Proprietor gained him the enmity of many, although he holds the deck courageously, and will fight as he ever fought, with his defiant flag floating at the peak....

Whew! Thatcher goes on with even greater glorification of his friend, knowing full well, I'm sure, that Orvis himself would shortly read the book. Also in Thatcher's book is the only description I've ever encountered of the *inside* of Orvis's store, which in the early 1900s was located in Manchester village near the Equinox:

...the Wayfarer...abruptly swung around on his heels and stepped within, a quick turn to the right through one of the vestibule doors bringing him into a large room formerly constituting the business portion of the bank.

Minnow buckets, and traps, creels of woven reed, loaded shells, base balls [sic] and bats, and tennis balls crowded the shelves to the right, and in the corners underneath, circular stands holding golf clubs, with the surplusage arranged against the walls, met his glance. He saw before him a show case filled with many things that delight the sportsman's soul, and back of this a case containing rods and gaffs, landing nets, reels and packages of flies, and hooks, and lines, and leaders ready for quick sale, and overtopping all stuffed trophies of field, and lake and stream. On the left ran a counter surmounted by a glass case, exhibiting a varied assortment of hunting knives, fly books, compasses, and all the little paraphernalia so necessary to the hunter and fisherman, and back of this again rifles and shot guns found glass covered lodgement. This was the showroom belonging to the maker of fishing rods, the best in America, and in the esteem of the newcomer, the best in the world. To this occupation had been added the art of fly tying, and manufacturing of flies to trick the salmon and delude the trout. Here could be found in stock all the conventional flies ever made, and many specimens made to the description and order of enthusiastic anglers, who intensely desired in all honesty to become skilled "Nature Fakirs [sic]."

Nearly in the center of the room was located a revolving stand of large photographs, showing many varied views of the choice fishing grounds of our country, the glass encased pictures being flanked on their borders by those special flies better suited to the killing of the fish that swam in their waters. This was a text book with which no fault could be found, for the most stolid could easily read and learn from its pages.

I was surprised to learn from Thatcher's description that Orvis was running what was apparently a general sporting-goods store — including golf and tennis — instead of selling only fishing tackle as I'd always supposed, although it makes perfect sense considering the diversity of Manchester's tourist trade and the relatively poor fishing in the nearby Battenkill. The panels of photographs and flies Thatcher mentions were assembled by Mary Ellen Orvis Marbury, Charles Orvis's daughter, for the 1893 World's Columbian Exposition at Chicago where they were part of an exhibit mounted by the U.S. Fish Commission. Other than their mention by Thatcher, I've seen no further record of those panels until 1968 when they were discovered in the attic of an old Orvis Manchester building and quickly became a centerpiece for the newly formed American Museum of Fly Fishing, where they remain on display.[39]

It was Marbury who compiled the massive and widely successful book *Favorite Flies and Their Histories*, published in 1892 and often reprinted over the years, which was a collection of fly patterns plus local history and lore from various angling corners of North America. Her book became widely famous for its lush color plates of contemporary fly patterns, following a style set in 1883 by the book *Fishing with the Fly*, a collection of angling anecdotes and advice from twenty-four authors that her father co-edited with his friend A. Nelson Cheney. She had only a brief marriage, ending in divorce, to John Marbury, and their only child died young. She seems otherwise to have thrown herself into the various Orvis family enterprises and managed the company's thriving fly-tying department between 1876 and 1904. The few fragments of her life that are known offer a tantalizing combination of personal tragedy and professional creativity, but there's so little information available that a full biography will probably never be possible.

Mary Orvis Marbury died at Manchester in 1914, and her father Charles died shortly thereafter in 1915. Their passing coincided with the end of a major period in American angling, for by 1915 the days

Mary Ellen Orvis Marbury. *Photo courtesy AMFF.*

of wild brook trout, colorful wet flies, and wilderness waters were all but over. After the widely traveled angling author and editor Charles Hallock of New York visited his friend Orvis at Manchester in 1882, he wrote a great deal about Orvis, his factory, and the beauty of Manchester, and very little about trout fishing in the nearby Batten-kill.[40] It is somehow ironic that by 1856 when Orvis started making tackle, the banner years of Battenkill brook trout were already long gone, and that after the Civil War the region's highly touted trout fishing became almost entirely dependent on hatchery fish.

The hatchery culture of American brook trout had its beginnings at Cleveland, Ohio, in 1853, when Theodatus Garlick and H. A. Ackley began experimenting with some Lake Superior strains, although hatcheries for other fish had been known in western Europe since the mid-fifteenth century. By the 1850s, our brook-trout fishing had been devastated by declines in habitat quality and by overfishing, and in 1852 George Perkins Marsh delivered a report commissioned by the Vermont Legislature, which in part suggested that the recent havoc wrought on brook-trout populations could be at least partly remedied by fish hatcheries.

The well-known Seth Green had started his commercial hatchery in western New York by 1864, largely in response to rapidly increasing market prices for brook trout, which at the time were selling to hotels and restaurants for as much as a dollar per pound. This high price gave rise to a profusion of small, private hatcheries over the next two decades, which had the combined effect of driving prices down and making large numbers of hatchery brookies available for stocking streams at relatively low prices. The establishment of the U.S. Fish Commission in 1872, the same year as General Grant's election to a second presidential term, put the federal government in the hatchery business as well, often supplying fish — including brook trout — for stocking under the auspices of various state fish commissions. Vermont finally built its first state hatchery at Roxbury in 1890, although private hatcheries in the region — notably at Bennington — were also supplying the Battenkill with trout considerably before that date.

The earliest record of stocking the Battenkill that I've seen refers to brook trout having been planted in 1876 in White Creek, a major Battenkill tributary at Salem, New York.[41] Brook-trout stocking in the main river may have started at about the same time or slightly earlier, but probably not before 1870. By the 1880s, stocking was extensive. The Vermont State Fish Commissioner's biannual report for 1889–1890 notes that 40,000 brookies had recently been stocked in the Battenkill between Manchester and Arlington.[42]

Bill Herrick on the big water below Shushan, where brown trout were apparently first introduced to the Battenkill between 1910 and 1920.

Brown trout were another matter. It's common knowledge among anglers that browns were first imported to New York from Germany in 1883, and most people have blithely assumed that their introduction was subsequently widespread and almost instantaneous. A number of early stockings quickly showed, however, that brown trout would apparently compete with brookies to the latter's detriment, and brown trout became unpopular among many anglers. To a degree, both the U.S. Fish Commission and various state commissions put the brakes on brown-trout distribution fairly quickly. In a 1914 report, Vermont's Fish and Game Commissioner noted that "the brown trout is propagated in very limited numbers incidental to having a few adults in stock for exhibition purposes. Care is taken to limit its distribution in waters where it will not destroy the native brook trout."

By this time, however, brown trout had apparently been stocked in the lower river of New York. The earliest reference I've found to Battenkill brown trout was in 1922, when a Vermont report noted plans to establish a brown-trout stripping station at Arlington, which refers to the removal of eggs and sperm from mature fish for hatchery production. This would apparently have depended on the capture of browns moving up from the lower river to spawn in the fall. While brown trout were being stocked by the state elsewhere in Vermont as early as 1896, the first documented reference I've found regarding brown-trout stockings in the Vermont Battenkill was in 1930 when 7,500 [German] brown trout and 5,550 Loch Levens [Scottish-strain brown trout][43] were stocked in the Green River and Warm Brook, Battenkill tributaries in Arlington and Sandgate. In 1932, and again according to early state fisheries reports, some 19,000 yearling brown trout were stocked in the Battenkill mainstream of Vermont, a process that was continued to varying degrees until the 1970s when stocking was halted and streambred fish became dominant.

Contrary to widespread belief, which holds the date to be much earlier, brown trout were not well established in the Battenkill until about 1935. That brown trout were then thriving is an understatement. Consider this notable catch as reported by a local newspaper on July 11, 1936:

> The largest trout ever taken from the Battenkill River in this vicinity was caught back of King's Laundry at Manchester Depot last evening by William Stuart of that village. The fish was of the brown variety and weighed exactly eight pounds and six ounces, nearly one pound more than the previous record of seven and one half pounds. The fish was taken with an ordinary steel rod and line, and Mr. Stuart had little difficulty in landing his catch.[44]

The river's largest-ever brown trout was taken at about the same time; a twelve-pound, two-ounce monster landed by young Roy Brown who was using a worm in the deep, dark Dutchman's Hole near the Vermont-New York border in 1930. Old regional fishing photographs from the 1930s and 1940s show an extraordinary number of very large brown trout, which have been speculated about at length by modern anglers who rarely see such fish these days. Given the relatively recent introduction of browns to the river, the temporary abundance of large fish is in retrospect no surprise. It was in many respects typical of a predator's response to a new, food-rich environment. Brown trout are fierce aquatic predators, with larger ones acting much like solitary underwater wolves, and many of them grew rapidly in their new Battenkill surroundings—fed partly and unwittingly by generous stockings of small brook trout—until brown trout populations began to stabilize in the 1950s and the numbers of extremely large trout declined.

The 1930s were watershed years for the Battenkill valley, specifically marking a transition that extends far beyond the establishment of brown trout. By 1938, the tackle business founded by Charles Orvis was on the rocks, having only two employees: Bert Orvis and the last in Orvis's long line of lady fly tiers, Hallie Thompson Galaise. The grand Equinox Hotel went bankrupt in those Depression years, the victim of a declining trade coupled with heavy debt assumed in construction of an 18-hole golf course for the hotel adjacent to the slightly older and private Ekwanok course. Dorset's once great marble industry had faded by 1917, and the last large marble mill on the upper 'Kill at Manchester was closed in 1932. One by one, many of the region's small manufacturing, saw-, and other mills were closed in a pattern that was repeated from Manchester downriver to Greenwich, New York, and beyond. It was a bleak interval.

Yet in that same period, some things changed for the better, including the Battenkill, which after almost two centuries of extraordinary abuse was gradually becoming cleaner. Manchester, for example, had been piping domestic sewage directly into the river after about 1900, but in 1935 construction was started on the town's first sewage-treatment plant. A gradual decrease in the number of active mills helped the river and its tributaries to cleanse themselves slowly of sawdust and other waste, and the legislative creation of the adjacent Green Mountain National Forest in 1932 brought some watershed protection to the river's high, eastern tributaries. In 1939, Dudley Clark "Duckie" Corkran, who was first attracted to Manchester by its golf courses, bought the nearly defunct Orvis Company, bringing it to a new prosperity through the 1950s and early 1960s. And in 1938, Fred Pabst began developing rope tows and

One of many outstanding temple-form Green-revival-style homes built along the lower river between 1810 and the Civil War, an era when there was big money in sheep. This house is in Argyle, NY, which town is the source of numerous lower-river tributaries.

downhill skiing at Bromley, which was the beginning of what came to be a multimillion dollar ski industry in the mountains surrounding the upper Battenkill.

During the same period in the lower valley of New York, all of the clocks stopped. They are still stopped. In driving through the towns of Salem, Jackson, Greenwich, and Easton along the lower river, I often have the eerie feeling of having stepped back in time to about 1950 or perhaps a little earlier. Here I see few houses built after that date, and the area's most prominent architectural features are lovely Greek Revival-style homes that date back to the pre-Civil War days when there was big money in sheep. Many of the old mills are still standing as silent ruins. Farming still dominates the landscape, which other than newer tractors and shiny silos looks much as it must have looked fifty or more years ago. Real estate prices have long been depressed, there are at least a few empty storefronts in almost every commercial center, and the busy, urban worlds of Albany and Glens Falls on the Hudson seem a million miles distant rather than a scant thirty as the crow flies. The primary difference has been — and remains — the development of tourism in the upper valley and the absence of tourism or developing industry in the lower, and by 1940 these still prevalent differences were firmly established.

There was a renaissance of sorts along the upper Battenkill during the 1940s, a rapid influx of painters and illustrators that was remarkable for its breadth. Some of these men, such as Jack Atherton, eventually became better known as fishermen. Others, most notably Norman Rockwell, achieved widespread fame for their wryly humorous depictions of everyday life in small towns along the river. At one time in the late 1940s there were four illustrators living in Arlington who were all painting covers for the *Saturday Evening Post* as well as illustrating a wide variety of other contemporary magazines and books. Lee Wulff is the fifth man I include in this group, and at that time he was just beginning a career in writing and film-making that eventually brought him international fame as a sportsman.

Everything happened almost at once. In the spring of 1939, Norman and Mary Rockwell moved from New Rochelle, New York, to Arlington, Vermont, near the Battenkill. Meade Schaeffer, another illustrator who had known Rockwell casually in New Rochelle, moved to Arlington in 1940. Lee Wulff, than a commercial artist, moved his family in the fall of 1940 from Chappaqua to Shushan, New York, a few miles downstream from West Arlington. Jack Atherton, yet another illustrator, moved from Ridgefield, Connecticut, to West Arlington near both Rockwell and Schaeffer in 1941. Finally, George Hughes, still another *Post* illustrator, moved to Arlington in 1946 from New York City. Each of these men knew at least one of the others before moving to the region, and for three of them — Atherton, Schaeffer, and Wulff — the Battenkill's trout fishing was a major attraction.

The late Norman Rockwell is arguably the most popular American painter who ever lived. That his many *Post* covers and other work are more often known as illustration than as fine art has proved immaterial in terms of his wide reputation as an artist. His paintings of ordinary people doing ordinary things, often with some mild humor somehow injected, were a sweet and sentimental syrup; trite, cliched, and absolutely, totally wonderful. It was during his Arlington years along the Battenkill, which lasted from 1939 to 1953 when he moved to Stockbridge, Massachusetts, that much of his best work was produced, including the famous *Four Freedoms*.

For all of its sentimentality, most of Rockwell's work managed to be utterly genuine, an attribute he found in abundance among his Battenkill valley neighbors. Susan Meyer, in her 1981 book *Norman Rockwell's People*, gave this still-accurate description of the relationship between Rockwell and his adopted Vermont:

> In Vermont Rockwell found the environment he needed to concentrate totally on his pictures, a quiet and stable schedule for painting. What he also found was a community whose way of life most closely approximated the scenes he painted, a rural atmosphere where living is more clearly rooted to the universal themes of growing up and growing old. Rockwell didn't have to search far for ideas and subjects; they were all around him in Vermont...This was the world Norman Rockwell had depicted long before he laid eyes on Arlington...[45]

That Rockwell happened to settle in Arlington was an accident. In looking around southern Vermont, he first went up the Battenkill to Dorset, which by the late 1930s was becoming well settled as a quiet

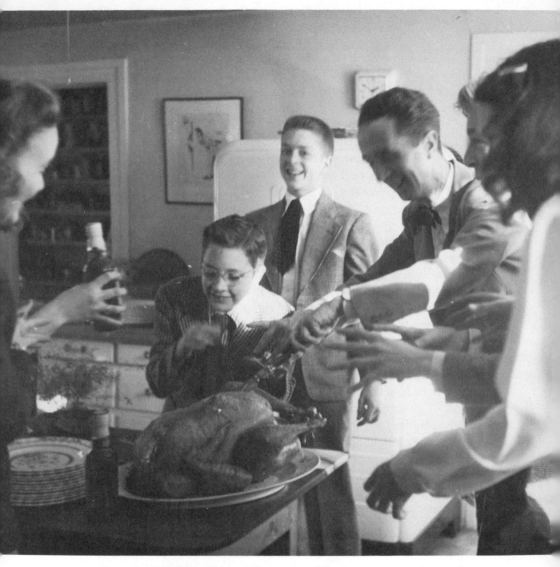

Norman Rockwell carving a turkey at West Arlington during the 1940s. Others in the photo include his sons and members of the Atherton and Schaeffer families. *Photo courtesy Atherton Collection/AMFF.*

retreat for old money. He tells that story in his autobiography, written in the late 1950s with his son Thomas and full of the same kind of light humor that marked his paintings.

So Mary and I drove up to Vermont to look at farms...In Bennington, we met a couple who said they'd show us around. But it was hard-cider season and they began to stop at every roadside stand and pretty soon were wildly soused...In Dorset a flouncy real-estate woman told us, "Oh you'll *love* Dorset. There isn't a single afternoon you won't go to a cocktail party. And we have po-*lo*, and golf." I looked at Mary, she nodded, and we excused ourselves. "I agree," said Mary..."Let's go back to the peaceful suburbs. I've had enough of the raucous country."

Arlington even now is a quiet village by-passed by many tourists en route to Manchester and the mountains a few miles north. The Rockwells stopped to spend the night on the way home, were charmed by the village during an evening walk, and on the next morning signed purchase papers for a small farm near the Battenkill. Rockwell was an acute student of human nature, a facility that greatly enhanced his paintings, and as he came to know his neighbors offered a characterization that even now should be reprinted and handed to incoming tourists:

The people we met were rugged and self-contained. None of that sham "I am so GLAD to know you!" accompanied by radiant smiles. They shook my hand, said, "How do," and waited to see how I'd turn out. Not hostile but reserved with a dignity and personal integrity which are rare in suburbia, where you're familiar with someone before you know him. In Vermont you earn the right to be called by your first name.

The relatively quiet, unassuming Rockwell made friends among several neighbors fairly quickly, many of whom soon became models for his paintings. It's significant that Rockwell ceased using professional models after leaving New Rochelle, finding among his Vermont friends a spark of reality that no professional model can mimic. When he needed a country doctor, for example, he painted the late Dr. George Russell of Arlington. Among Rockwell's famous *Four Freedoms* paintings is *Freedom of Speech*, which shows a plainly dressed, ordinary man standing and speaking his mind at a clearly rural town meeting. It is a simple and powerful work, drawn from such meetings Rockwell attended near the upper Battenkill where he witnessed democracy in its purest form. It is also a reincarnation of the many myths surrounding Ethan Allen, a declaration of individual rights and liberties that will be defended down to the last bit of gran-

Artist Meade Schaeffer on a Canadian-salmon trip he made with Jack Atherton in the
1940s. *Photo courtesy Atherton Collection/AMFF.*

ite in our stony soil. This sounds cliched, which it is, but Rockwell found it true in his little town. And it still is.

In 1943, shortly after he'd finished work on the *Freedoms*, Rockwell's studio burned. He and Meade Schaeffer had gone to hear Lee Wulff speak that night at a local high school, which I suspect was Wulff's way of trying out the new fishing and hunting films that he was then just starting to produce. Wulff joined Schaeffer and Rockwell afterward for a late conversation in the latter's studio, and Rockwell later blamed the fire on ashes carelessly knocked from his well-known pipe as the three were leaving the studio near midnight. A few days later, Rockwell bought his second Arlington home, on the green at West Arlington just over the red covered bridge that spans the Battenkill, where he had Walt Squires, a local carpenter, build a new studio behind the house. Rockwell painted here until 1953, when his wife's failing health prompted their move south to Stockbridge, apparently to be closer to whatever treatment facilities Mary Rockwell required.

Rockwell's move was probably also influenced by the breaking up of the small community of artists that he had inadvertently helped to create. The Schaeffers were close Rockwell friends—almost family— but moved away from Arlington in 1950. Atherton was equally close to Rockwell and died on a salmon-fishing trip in 1952. By the time Rockwell moved in 1953, the close-knit group of artists that had offered each other almost daily argument and support was gone. Rockwell remained at Stockbridge until his death in 1978.

Jack Atherton had more artistic dimensions than his friend Rockwell, but never became as well known for his art. Commercial art and illustration were a living for Atherton, while fine art was a life he took seriously. He painted numerous abstract works, some of which were collected by the Chicago Art Institute and by both the Modern and Metropolitan art museums in New York City. Atherton was said by Rockwell and others to be a perfectionist in all things from skiing to fishing to golf to art, an attribute that sometimes gave a stiff, draftsmanlike quality to his work.

Atherton and Rockwell were acquainted through the Illustrators Club in New York City, and it was at a downtown club meeting that Rockwell, who did not fish himself, first invited Atherton to fish the

Battenkill. Atherton moved north shortly thereafter with his family, building a starkly contemporary house along Route 313 in West Arlington overlooking the Battenkill. It's still the only "modern" home in the vicinity, presently painted dark brown and contrasting strongly with the white clapboards and green shutters marking most valley homes, and is easily spotted from the highway.

In moving from Ridgefield to Arlington, Atherton was escaping the hard-drinking, fast-track life of a New York City suburb, seeking not only a better working environment but also the then-excellent fishing on the Battenkill. He brought his intensity with him, however, and was widely known as often irritable. Although he was an ardent defender of his friend Rockwell's work, Atherton's sense of fine art could also be offended by Rockwell's overt sentimentality. As an example, here's an anecdote recalled by Rockwell several years after Atherton's death:

> I remember once I was painting the annual Boy Scout calendar, which I've done every year since about 1920. I went over to his [Atherton's] house. After we'd talked about miscellaneous subjects for a bit he asked, "What are you working on now?" "Oh, you don't want to know, Jack," I said, for I knew how he despised the Boy Scout calendar. "Yes I do," he said, visibly preparing himself for the worst. "All right," I said, "I'm doing the Boy Scout calendar." He moaned and began to crush the fingers of his right hand in his left. "Why do you do it?" he asked. "It's *propaganda*, it's sentimental trash. Why in God's name do you do it?" "Well, I *like* to do it," I said. He cracked his knuckles viciously and asked in a pained voice, "What's the subject?" "You don't want me to tell you, Jack," I said. "Yes, I do," he said. "What is it?" "A handsome one hundred percent American Boy Scout," I said, watching Jack begin to knead his skull furiously with his hands, "and a fine-looking upstanding American Cub Scout." "Oh, my *sweet* Judas," moaned Jack, swaying from side to side and wrapping his arms about his head. "What are they doing?" "You *don't* want to know," I said. "Yes, I do," he said. "Well, they're looking at something," I said. "What're they looking at?" he asked, gritting his teeth and groaning as if in actual physical torment. "Don't make me tell you," I said. "It'll kill you." "Tell me," he ranted. "Tell me." "They are looking," I said very distinctly. "at a cloudy vision of George Washington kneeling and praying in the snow at Valley Forge." Jack grunted horribly and grabbed at his neck, twisting about in his chair as if he'd been stabbed.[46]

Jack Atherton on West Arlington's Battenkill in the 1940s. *Photo courtesy Atherton Collection/AMFF.*

Atherton eventually became well known among trout fishermen for his 1951 book *The Fly and the Fish*, which he also illustrated. It was a carefully constructed and reasoned book on fly fishing for trout, much of which was based on his experiences with the Battenkill's then-abundant but notoriously difficult brown trout. His best-known contribution to angling, as described in his book, was in adding the color sensibilities and theories of a fine artist to the design of his widely effective trout flies.

After his 1952 death of a heart attack while salmon fishing in Canada, Atherton's cremated remains were returned to the Battenkill valley. He was buried next to a small maple tree on the riverbank near his home, with his widow Maxine, Lee Wulff, and a handful of others in attendance. There is no marker. But perhaps now, as then, the Battenkill will serve as such. I'll turn again to a Rockwell story that is not as careful a picture as Atherton would have wished but that's all the more valuable for its candor:

> Jack was a volatile man, exploding with a roaring, raging torrent of words and profanity at the slightest pretext...Late one afternoon, Schaef [Meade Schaeffer], Jack, and I were walking down to the Batten Kill [sic] River. The foam of the rapids was streaked with the gold and purple light of sunset, and the still pools mirrored the red clouds and darkening sky. Jack was fifteen or twenty feet ahead of Schaef and me and all of a sudden he stopped dead and began to curse violently and stamp his feet. Schaef and I rushed up and asked him what was the matter? "Just look at that blankety-blank blank damned river," said Jack. "Isn't that beautiful?" And he cursed some more.[47]

The aggressive, impetuous, and argumentative Lee Wulff. The careful, exacting, and irritable Jack Atherton. I know Atherton only by reputation and the accounts of his peers, but I came to know Lee Wulff very well in his later years. I have often wondered how these two men — neighbors and prominent anglers — got along with each other, and I've finally decided their relationship was cordial, respectful, and distant. During the years when I was publishing *Fly Rod & Reel* magazine and Wulff was writing the back-page column, I once suggested to Wulff that he write about Atherton. Wulff declined, noting Atherton was "a nice guy, but a one-river fisherman." This was a gently derisive comment within which I found apparent echoes of clashing egos almost forty years earlier. Jack mostly fished the Arlington water. Lee fished in Shushan, several miles downstream. There was probably not a pool in the entire river large enough to have held them both at once, at least not for very long.

By the time Lee Wulff died in 1991 at age eighty-six, he was unquestionably the world's best-known fisherman. His career of

writing, photography, film-making, and, eventually, television production spanned more than sixty years, during which time he was also
an ardent, effective, and often abrasive advocate of numerous conservation causes. He was born in Alaska in 1905, took an engineering
degree from Stanford, spent a year studying art in Paris, and by the
early 1930s was living in New York working as a freelance commercial artist and designing packaging for DuPont. At the same time he
was fishing, taking weekend trips to the Catskills or the Adirondacks
or — often — to the Battenkill. As I recall, he told me his first
Battenkill trip was in 1929, which he described in a 1940 magazine
article for *Country Life*:

> We stayed with old Merritt Russell in his big house in the fields with
> the locust trees around it and the most beautiful pool on the river a
> hundred yards behind it. I remember the spacious rooms with their
> high ceilings and the charm the old place had. We slept that night on
> real down mattresses and the blankets on one of the beds, fresh and
> clean though they were, still wore the leather straps and bells that
> graced them when they kept the Russell horses warm.[48]

The house Wulff mentions is presently the first large white house
on the left past the state rest area after one crosses the state line into
New York on Route 313 from Arlington. The pool behind the house
is a long, deep run against hemlock-covered ledges, now known as the
Grocery Pool. It's still a good spot for large trout.

By the early 1930s Wulff came frequently to the Battenkill on
weekends. He often fished with the late Al Prindle, who became postmaster at Shushan after Roosevelt was elected in 1932. Prindle was
immortalized, at least for local anglers, when the late Lew Oatman of
Shushan created the "Shushan Postmaster," a bucktail (trout fly) pattern that I've included in this book's fly-pattern appendix. In 1939
Wulff moved his then-new family from New York City to upstate
Chappaqua, and then to the Battenkill at Shushan in late 1940.
Shushan offered a quiet, pleasant village in a good school district,
relatively easy access to Manhattan by train or car, and excellent fishing. For Wulff, it was comfortable.

Although Wulff was taking occasional commercial art assignments
into the 1940s, he was by this time largely writing and filming hunting
and fishing. He was traveling widely, spending weeks at a time in

Lee Wulff in 1981.

northern Canada, which is part of the reason why he was never a close part of the Atherton-Rockwell group a few miles upriver. He and they were simply going in different directions. During the winter he was either writing, editing film, or often showing his films on the lecture circuit to groups such as the Chicago Executives Club, where he spoke annually for twenty-seven consecutive years. During this time he also acquired his first floatplane, which he was able to moor at one of several nearby ponds and that he quite literally used for commuting to Labrador and Newfoundland during the summer months for many years.

Wulff was by no means idolized or universally popular among local sportsmen. Although he mellowed a little in later years, as a younger man he could be extremely argumentative, forcefully expounding on whatever fishing or hunting theory he happened to hold dear at the time. Things often degenerated into a contest, usually proposed by Wulff, to see who could climb a mountain fastest, cast the farthest, and so forth. That Wulff often won such contests — either verbally or physically — reinforced his own sense of correctness, but didn't reinforce many friendships. I mention this as one of several reasons why I believe he eventually left the lower Battenkill, moving to Keene in south-central New Hampshire in 1961.

I was often told by Wulff that he left the 'Kill because the advent of spinning as a fishing method after World War II had increased the river's fishing pressure and decimated its population of large trout, which is something he also described often in print. Although I never bothered to argue the point with him, I don't believe things were that simple. For one thing, fishing of any kind in the Keene area ranges from mediocre to non-existent, which was as true then as it is now, so fishing wasn't the attraction. The Keene area did (and does) have an airport, and Wulff was able to find a home with an adjacent pasture for a grass landing strip, so he was somewhat closer by plane to his favored areas of northeastern Canada.

For another, by attributing his move to declining fishing caused by spinning, he was able to more dramatically make his point about the importance of catch-and-release angling, a position he took adamantly — and ultimately with wide success — from the 1930s until his death. It is true that Battenkill trout were getting smaller and fewer during the late 1950s, but spinning and the removal of greater numbers of trout from the river were only part of the reason. Brown-trout introductions in the 1920s and 1930s produced a temporarily large number of big brown trout that lasted approximately until the mid-1950s, after which populations of naturally reproducing browns began to stabilize and their average size declined naturally. Populations of naturally reproducing trout were further held down by continued stockings of hatchery fish, with which streambred fish had to compete for food and living space. Increasing numbers of new fishermen using new methods contributed to the decline, but they didn't create it.

Finally, Lee and Helen Wulff were divorced during his Battenkill years. As much as we talked of many things over the years, he mentioned this seldom. I gathered it was painful, none of my business, and I never asked further. When he finally moved to Keene, he went by himself. There was also a second and very brief failed marriage before he had the good fortune to meet Joan Salvato, herself a well-known angler and competitive caster, whom Wulff married for keeps in 1967. Joan and Lee moved from Keene to the upper Beaverkill in New York's Catskill Mountains in 1978 where they started a fly-fishing school featuring Joan's exceptional fly-casting instruction and Lee's ideas on trout-fishing tactics and flies. The school under Joan continues; Lee Wulff does not. He died of an apparent heart attack while at the controls of his airplane on April 28, 1991. Yes, that's an abrupt ending. But Lee was often like that.

CHAPTER 7

Changes, Conflicts, and Canoes

*D*uckie Corkran is remembered partly for his temper, which could be ferocious. He owned The Orvis Company at Manchester, Vermont, from 1939 until 1965, then lived in retirement here until his death in 1989 at age ninety-three. The last time I saw him driving his big Buick sedan, he was stuck behind a village matron who was hesitant about turning onto busy Route 7-A from the supermarket parking lot. Duckie honked his horn, his short form barely visible above the steering wheel as I waited in my own car behind him. He honked again, but no one moved. Finally he rolled down his window and screeched, "Get out of the way, you old bat!" Duckie swerved his car viciously from the exit into the entry lane, honked again as he darted past a line of waiting traffic, and went sweeping up the highway as other cars dodged to the right and left. I have often wanted to do the same thing, but I never had Duckie's nerve.

An Orvis Company promotional photograph from the 1950s. Duckie Corkran is at lower left, Wes Jordan at upper right. Local lore has this extraordinary catch coming from the Battenkill, but I think the privately stocked Equinox Trout Pond was the more likely source. *Photo courtesy AMFF.*

Duckie Corkran fishing the Battenkill in the early 1950s. *Photo courtesy AMFF.*

Fabled Orvis rodmaker Wesley D. Jordan. *Photo courtesy AMFF.*

It was that nerve, perhaps, and the same grim determination that made him such a successful, competitive golfer, that enabled Corkran to struggle through the war years with the nearly defunct Orvis Company he'd bought in 1939 with financial help from Bart Arkell, the founder of Beech-Nut Packing Company. Arkell was a long-time Manchester summer resident who for many years gave widely to a variety of causes, although his name is rarely associated with Orvis, within which he was a silent partner. It was, however, Arkell's money in combination with Corkran's considerable grit that allowed the company to survive and eventually to grow. Corkran and Orvis got through the early 1940s on U.S. Army orders for white-painted, split-bamboo ski poles used by the famous 10th Mountain Division in Colorado training, and on orders for a blown-glass minnow trap that Charles Orvis had designed many years before.

One of Corkran's first moves with Orvis — and probably his best — was to hire Wesley D. Jordan away from Indiana's South Bend Rod Company, where Jordan supervised the making of split-bamboo rods after having worked for a similar company in Massachusetts since 1919. Jordan was a fisherman and a superb mechanic, one of those rare people who could squint along a recalcitrant machine, pronounce it "a little more than straight," tap just the right spot with a hammer, and then pronounce it perfect. It was characteristic of Jordan's own pride and wry humor that he much later noted, as regards the finely arcane art of rod-building, that "anyone with a fifth-grade education and twenty years' experience can be a rodmaker." Jordan was re-building the old Orvis rod-shop machinery by 1941 and in 1950 was awarded a patent for the now-famous impregnation process that gave Orvis a substantial competitive edge in fly-rod manufacturing through the 1950s and 1960s. At a time when almost all other bamboo fly rods were finished with exterior coats of varnish, which meant they were both fragile and susceptible to water damage, Jordan was impregnating his glued-up bamboo sections with Bakelite, which produced a more durable rod.

The new rods were (and still are) successful, helped by endorsements from such popular angling writers as Joe Brooks and Lee Wulff, and in 1956 Corkran was able to build a new Orvis store and office, a red structure of shedlike design on Route 7-A less than a mile from where Charles Orvis had founded the company a hundred years before. Jordan died at age eighty-one in 1975, but the tradition he and Corkran helped to create is alive and well by the Battenkill. The greatly expanded Orvis store, offices, and rod shop still occupy the same site, and are still a mecca for sportsmen traveling the Northeast.

Corkran sold the company in 1965 to Leigh Perkins of Cleveland, *who* had bought his first Orvis rod in 1948 while attending Williams College in nearby northwestern Massachusetts, had both hunted and fished in the area, and *who* Dick Finlay introduced to Duckie. Finlay is also a Williams graduate who, as it happens, was using Orvis ski poles in training with the 10th Mountain Division in the 1940s and who later moved from New Jersey to join Orvis as a rod-building trainee in 1947. The company grew dramatically under Perkins, who —like Corkran and Charles Orvis before him—was able to use his exceptional marketing skills to capitalize on both the idea of an upscale country life and the cachet of Vermont to sell a wide variety of goods in addition to fishing tackle. Catalog mailings went from the thousands to hundreds of thousands and into the millions over the years, product lines diversified, and Orvis grew enormously.

During the last few years of his life, Duckie used to call me about once every two weeks, usually on Thursdays around four o'clock. At the time I was working as the director of the American Museum of Fly Fishing, and Corkran would announce in his sharp, raspy voice that he had something to donate to the collection and that I'd better come over for a drink and check it out. So I'd go over and sit with Duckie on his back porch, visiting for an hour or two about the tackle-business old days, which Duckie enjoyed a great deal. I did, too, of course, although Duckie kept up his donation pretext — instead of simply inviting me over — until both he and the tackle were gone.

Corkran maintained a keen interest in Orvis long after he'd sold it, which sale Leigh Perkins once described figuratively as being like marrying Duckie's daughter (Corkran had no children). One afternoon, after one of many effusive magazine articles in the 1980s about Orvis had described the Perkins family as living the image of a baronial country life, Duckie was shaking his head in wonder at the idea of "Lord Orvis." I remember telling Duckie about my correspondence with a tackle collector in France who wrote beginner's

Leigh Perkins, Sr., who bought Orvis in 1965.

English and who had consequently sent me a letter addressed to "Sir John Merwin." The next afternoon, as I explained to Duckie, I had gone to the Perkins's home on some business, flourished that envelope, and asked Romi (Mrs. Leigh) Perkins to please tell "Lord Orvis" that "Sir John" had arrived. Duckie laughed for a long time over that, not only for the moment's humor, but with great satisfaction at what his once-little company had become.

The Battenkill in both Vermont and New York has been promoted widely as a trout stream since before the Civil War. The Orvis Company in its various incarnations for almost 150 years has been foremost among those promoters, linking its commercial image logically enough to the river's natural beauty and to its trout fishing. Yet through much of that time, the river's wide reputation has far exceeded its fishing. This is true at present and was equally true in the supposed glory years of trout fishing here in the late 1800s, which prove not to have been so great when looked at closely.

In recent years as pressure on the river from various user groups has increased, much to the concern of local residents up and down the valley, there has been a growing tendency to blame Orvis for the river's seemingly sudden popularity and crowding. The question is hardly that simple, and the verbal Orvis-bashing that's become increasingly popular downstream is both inaccurate and unfair. No, I don't work for Orvis and have no wish to be their apologist, but I

Manchester's Orvis store as it appeared in the early 1980s.

hope to make it obvious that blaming Orvis for many of the river's current problems diverts attention from what some of the problems *really* are and how some of them might be resolved.

First, almost every motel, hotel, restaurant, and other business near the river from its Dorset headwaters to the Hudson uses the river somehow in commercial promotion with words such as "near the famous Battenkill" or others to that effect. This ranges from selling "Equinox on the Battenkill" condominiums at Manchester to "Camping on the Battenkill" at Arlington all the way downstream to the Battenkill Country Club on the river at Greenwich, New York. You can buy a baseball glove at Battenkill Sports, rent a boat at Battenkill Canoe, or go to buy clothing in Battenkill Plaza. I don't know if there's a Battenkill Pizza yet, but if not there will be. In this respect, the river runs as a thread through the region's entire commercial fabric, which is hardly dominated by a single company, even a nationally prominent one such as Orvis.

In spite of its obvious importance, and in spite of all the casual attention it gets in brochures for motels and gift shops, the river is surprisingly neglected, being generally taken for granted by those who live or travel in its valley. One reason, and probably the most important one, is because the river is presently cleaner and generally in a better natural condition than at any time in the past two centuries. This is primarily because of the region's changing economy. The sheep-raising bonanza that caused so much land clearing before the Civil War is long over, and most of the region has become naturally reforested. The nineteenth-century sawmills that once dumped tons of sawdust into the mainstream and its tributaries are gone, too, as are almost all of the old dams that provided power for these and other mills. The Battenkill is now free-flowing without dams between the old mill dam in downtown Manchester for thirty-four miles downstream to one of the remaining dams at Greenwich, New York, near the Hudson.

During the late 1960s and 1970s, which is about the same time that the last midreach, main-stream dams were naturally washing away, increased federal funding for sewage-treatment plants brought newly upgraded plants to several towns along the river. Environmentally sensitive legislation passed at state and federal levels during the 1970s coupled with increasingly restrictive local zoning brought further improvements and protection. Now both domestic and municipal wastes are no longer a serious problem and water quality has substantially improved.

The banning of DDT in 1972 and subsequent intensive regulation governing the use of other environmentally persistent pesticides has also caused substantial improvement. Such chemicals were widely used on everything from golf courses to lawns to farms to forest lands after World War II, and those fisherman who complained of diminishing aquatic-insect hatches during the 1950s and 1960s might best have blamed the unseen effects of pesticides. Although such effects have never been formally demonstrated in the Battenkill, they undoubtedly existed, and only in the past twenty years has the river been undergoing its own slow and natural recovery.

A new environmental awareness over the past two decades brought battles to the Battenkill as it did elsewhere. On the lower river was an intense, often acrimonious fight in the 1970s involving Trout Unlimited and other conservation groups, New York state authorities, and a company called Biotech Mills on the river at Battenville (in Greenwich). The mill was eventually closed, and both trout habitat and water quality at Battenville became much improved.[49]

Other problems have been more recent. During the late 1980s a company known as Vicon proposed dumping toxic ash, generated by regional garbage incineration performed elsewhere, at a landfill less than a hundred yards from the Battenkill's banks in Sunderland. Local and regional opposition was widespread and vigorous, Vicon eventually went bankrupt, and the plan was dropped, at least for the time being. Meanwhile, the old landfill remains, no longer used for private or municipal dumping but not yet formally closed or capped with the addition of final test wells to monitor in ongoing fashion what leaches into groundwater after decades of continuous dumping. The landfill was in existence long before many environmentally hazardous materials became intensively regulated, and no one really knows what it contains or what might appear in adjacent ground water ten, twenty, or fifty years from now. It is — potentially, at least — an ecological time bomb.

For all of the many improvements in the river over the past few decades, three major problem areas remain, each of which has environmental overtones but is more social and political in nature.

The Battenkill's shallow, slow flow makes for difficult, skittish trout.

These pertain to trout habitat and angling regulations, which are generally archaic; conflicts among rapidly growing user groups, notably canoeists and fishermen; and river access, which is now almost unrestricted but is gradually shrinking. All of these questions have become contentious in recent years and will likely becomes more so in the future.

While the Battenkill's water quality is excellent, its physical trout habitat is generally poor. The river produces far fewer trout naturally than would be possible if physical habitat conditions were improved. This is not difficult for many fishermen to understand. Unfortunately, it is perhaps beyond belief to the non-fishing public, who see an ap-

parently pristine river known for its trout fishing and thus assume —
incorrectly — that the Battenkill's trout fishery is as productive as
the river itself appears. Because the river's water quality is excellent and because there's an abundance of spawning habitat for adults
and nursery areas for young trout, the primary factor limiting numbers of trout is apparently a lack of overhead cover, which essentially
means places where trout hide from predators when not actively
feeding.

Yes, trout hide under rocks, and many trout rivers of steep gradient and a correspondingly fast current have plentiful large boulders
around and under which trout seek shelter. But because of the
Battenkill's generally low gradient and slow flow, its riverbed is
comprised mainly of smooth, golfball- to softball-size cobbles and
stones, or even just coarse sand or silt in areas of slower current. It
should be evident to anyone who looks at one of the river's long, still
pools in summer low water that hiding places for trout among the
bottom rocks are scarce; the rocks are just too small.

Other trout streams of low gradient and slow flow often have
water plants such as *Elodea* growing profusely, clumps of which offer
trout shelter in the absence of large rocks or other hiding spots.
There are a few spots in the Battenkill, such as Sunderland's Hill
Farm stretch, where water plants grow abundantly enough to serve as
shelter. But for the most part, the 'Kill's current is just fast enough to
prevent widespread growth of rooted aquatic plants but not fast
enough to expose large boulders in the riverbed. Trout shelter that
would otherwise be provided is thus conspicuously absent.

Historically, the Battenkill's trout depended on woody debris in
the river for shelter — fallen trees, stumps, logjams, and the like that
accumulated in the river over long periods and provided abundant
cover. While such debris was washed away by an occasional flood, it
was continually being replenished by trees falling in from heavily
wooded riverbanks and by similar material washing downstream in
high water. With the extensive land clearing in the region that started
during the 1760s and reached a peak by 1840, woody debris that
washed away in floods was no longer being re-supplied from
now-barren riverbanks, and the river's ability to support numerous
trout declined. While the river's water quality has been substantially
restored in recent decades, its physical trout habitat has not. The

State and federal workers placing a trout-habitat-improvement structure in the 'Kill at West Arlington in 1992.

result is a lovely and sparkling river that supports far fewer trout than would be possible if instream cover were abundant.

The importance of cover has been measured within the Battenkill itself. In conducting ongoing trout population studies, Vermont biologists have been comparing different river sections while at the same time noting the degree of cover in each. According to their reports, one brushy river stretch near Manchester with abundant logs and overhanging brush is holding *seven times more* trout per acre of stream than the popular, open river section in West Arlington where overhead and instream cover is scarce.[50] Using a "per acre" measurement is a little misleading because even though the West Arlington section is about four times wider than the Manchester section, there is little or no cover (and few trout) at midstream in the larger water. However, even when converted to linear measure (trout per mile) and disregarding stream width, the brushy, log-strewn Manchester water still shows about *twice* the number of trout. From my own experience, there are many more large brown and brook trout in the brushy, upstream water.

Part of the difference derives from fishing pressure, which is intense at West Arlington and less so at Manchester because the latter is more difficult to fish. But I believe much of the difference is attributable to cover or lack of same simply because the local data generally parallel more exhaustive studies performed elsewhere. Wisconsin natural-resource agencies have long been national leaders in stream improvement. In certain instances of intensive stream-improvement work — adding overhead cover by various means — Wisconsin researchers have demonstrated a *ten-fold* increase in numbers of wild trout within a few years after a project's completion.[51] The comparison is especially appealing because many of Wisconsin's better trout streams are of generally low gradient, much like the Battenkill. The Wisconsin programs were so successful that the state ultimately developed a trout stamp, sold in conjunction with fishing licenses, revenues from which are used solely for stream-habitat enhancement in much the same way that federal duck-stamp sales finance habitat improvement for waterfowl.

Vermont's long-term emphasis in managing its trout streams has been on regulation coupled with habitat protection, both of which are necessary but obviously not enough. There's been little — if any — emphasis placed on stream-habitat improvement, which puts our state decades behind New York, Wisconsin, and others that have been progressive in this regard. The Battenkill, especially, could benefit dramatically from a long-term stream-improvement program, but such programs don't yet appear to be a major component of Vermont's trout-fishing future.

Part of the problem is money. Stream-improvement structures first need to be carefully designed, and then often require heavy equipment for the placing of large rocks or other material. Substantial hand labor is also usually involved. Most state budgets — including Vermont's — simply can't accommodate the addition of such programs at present, but there is another way. In the fall of 1992 a small start was made along the Arlington Battenkill when a few habitat-improvement structures were placed in a cooperative project that started with private funds. Dick Finlay of Manchester, perhaps the most devoted of several volunteers who work for the river's benefit, headed an effort that brought the Town of Arlington, state fisheries officials, the Soil Conservation Service, and the Forest Service together in a project that married the town's need to repair a riverside road with the river's need for habitat work. Dick, I, and others worked at raising private contributions to supplement Arlington highway funds. The several thousand dollars raised qualified for a federal matching grant, and the river ultimately got four dollars worth of work for every dollar we raised. It was a long bureaucratic journey, but was well worth it. The town was able to repair its road, and the river's trout fishing benefitted at the same time. It was a significant first step for Vermont in modern stream-improvement on the Battenkill where there's much, much more to be done.

The question extends far beyond mere trout fishing and fishermen. There never has been any study of the Battenkill's direct contribution to the regional economy, measured in terms of dollars spent by fishermen and other river users, but the river's economic influence in Vermont and New York combined unquestionably runs to a million or more dollars annually. When I drive along the river to fish, I buy sandwiches, coffee, and gasoline at local stores en route. If I came from out of state for the fishing — as many do — I would also buy fishing tackle, one or more fishing licenses, motel rooms, restaurant meals, and probably some unrelated items at a number of local stores. Alphonse Gilbert, a resource economist at the University of Vermont, recently estimated the annual economic benefit of sport-fishing in Vermont at $104 million.[52] A similar study of the Battenkill region would be enlightening, if only because it would open the eyes of many non-anglers whose livelihoods are indirectly but substantially enhanced by the river itself. Simply stated, anything that improves the river's trout fishing will likewise enhance local businesses. This is only common sense and should be evident even though no regional economic studies have been made.

There is a widespread perception among anglers that the Battenkill's trout fishing "isn't what it used to be." That commonly used phrase may be more indicative of selective memories, recalling only those days past when fish were caught, than of actual fishing conditions. For example, according to a Vermont Fish and Game report published back in the good old days of 1934:

> The Battenkill is one of the most famous trout streams of the state, and Vermont boosters usually devote considerable time to describing the merits of the stream whenever the subject of trout fishing is under discussion. A qualifying statement is usually added, however, to the effect that the stream "isn't what it used to be."

It's almost certain that "what used to be" never really was, at least in the memory of any living angler. The Battenkill's once-virgin brook trout fishing was in decline by 1810 or earlier. During the period from the late 1920s through the late 1950s, when the river was first being stocked with hatchery brown trout and when large brown trout were temporarily abundant, the catch rate — meaning trout caught per hour of angling effort — was almost the same as it is now: an average of about 0.5 trout per hour.[53]

By 1976 Vermont decided to manage the Battenkill as a wild-trout fishery, and the stocking of hatchery brown and brook trout was halted. Natural reproduction was more than adequate, and it made little sense to spend several dollars to produce a pound of hatchery trout when the river at no cost would produce trout better adapted to living in the wild. At this point it had taken almost a hundred years to realize the maxim stated by Vermont's fish and game commissioners when the state's first trout hatchery was opened in 1890:

A sunny afternoon on the West Arlington water.

> If there is a profit to the state in the artificial propagation of fish, there is vastly more profit in securing conditions which will permit natural propagation.

Unfortunately, Vermont's ongoing wild-trout management of the Battenkill hasn't been accompanied by a change in angling regulations, although that may change slightly if newly proposed regulations for a short river stretch are adopted for 1993. As a general case, Vermont's regulatory approach to wild-trout streams has been — and is — archaic. The intensively fished wild-trout Battenkill is now managed under the same liberal creel limits that apply both to the state's most remote beaver bogs and to its most heavily stocked trout streams elsewhere. Even a non-fisherman must scratch her or his head at this lack of logic; as a fisherman, I find it absurd.

On closer examination, things get worse instead of better. Current general regulations as they apply to the Vermont Battenkill favor an introduced species — brown trout — at the expense of brook trout that have been native to the river for thousands of years. Brown trout today outnumber brook trout by about nine to one in the popular West Arlington water along Route 313. At the same time, extensive creel surveys have shown consistently that brook trout, which are in general easier to catch than brown trout, are caught in numbers disproportionate to their presence in the overall trout population and are being removed from the stream at a faster rate than brown trout.

The disproportionate harvest of a more easily caught trout species has become a wide concern in the American west regarding streams holding native cutthroat trout in some combination with introduced browns, rainbows, or brook trout. The native cutthroats, being the most gullible, are caught at a faster rate than other trout species in the same rivers when managed under catch limits that don't differentiate among trout species. Because native cutthroats in many western streams are the object of ongoing preservation programs aimed at indigenous species, the regulatory problem is a serious one.

The same thing is happening on Vermont's Battenkill, although the importance of brook trout as a native species here doesn't seem to have captured anyone's attention yet. On the contrary. For 1993 Vermont has adopted a new statewide trout-fishing rule that keeps the daily creel limit at twelve trout of which *no more than six* may be browns or rainbows. This rule was apparently designed to spread the catch of hatchery trout in stocked streams over a greater time period. It should no longer be possible to follow the state stocking truck to a bridge and quickly catch a dozen browns fresh from the holding tanks; now you can take only six per day.

For streams that are stocked, I suppose the new rule makes some sense. But for heavily fished wild-trout streams such as the Battenkill where brown and brook trout have a tenuous coexistence, the rule is a myopic disaster. It places additional pressure on already declining stocks of wild brook trout, which as *the* native species deserves better treatment. Politics as practiced in Montpelier, Vermont's capitol city, and fisheries management often have been strange bedfellows, but no longer. In this case, at least, sound management has been shoved from the bed completely.

Through all of this it can be argued that the presently high creel limits are immaterial on the Battenkill. The river's fishing is so difficult that catching a dozen trout in a day's outing is rare, although occasionally it's accomplished by skilled anglers. But that's not the point. In setting regulations, the state is declaring its management *intent*. As a resident and concerned angler, I find that intent as presently stated to be an embarrassment.

There is some small hope. After several decades of squabbles and antiquated management of the state's trout fisheries, Vermont fish and wildlife officials are finally beginning to proceed in a methodical, modern manner. A massive statewide angler survey was conducted recently to determine angler attitudes and preferences regarding both cold- and warmwater fisheries. One result is a forthcoming statewide trout-management plan now scheduled for release in the spring of 1993. Locally, more restrictive angling regulations were proposed by the state in 1992 for a short reach of the West Arlington Battenkill on a test basis. Specifically, the daily creel limit would have been reduced from twelve to three trout, a so-called "slot limit" established under which all trout between ten and fourteen inches would have to be released unharmed, and fishermen would be restricted to artificial lures and flies only.

Some local opposition to the proposed rules was highly vocal. At a public hearing held by the state to explain its plans, landowners threatened to post their land. Others cried that fishing was being

Landing a trout under the Route 313 highway bridge, Shushan.

stolen "from the children." Still others extolled the virtues of local control and, as usual, cursed the state for trying to horn in on the town's affairs. There were self-anointed authorities in the crowd who declared the biologists' data to be wetter than the river itself and others who loudly blamed the Orvis Company in Manchester for encouraging too many fishermen on the Battenkill. The whole affair had the illogical atmosphere of a lynch mob in which few, if any, people actually *listened* to the state's presentation. As one person said to me afterward, "If the state had been trying to give money away, no one there would have taken it."

One can only hope the state will eventually persevere. District fisheries biologists who research the Vermont Battenkill have collected more than enough careful data to justify at least a test of increasingly restrictive regulations. The fishing in the river can be much improved. And the area's economy will benefit as a result.

The New York experience has some parallels to what's now happening in Vermont, although progressive management changes on New York's lower Battenkill were enacted more than twenty years ago. By the mid-1950s fishermen along the lower river were complaining of an apparent reduction in trout numbers and size. In response to a number of regional meetings New York began trout-population studies and creel surveys, stocked a large number of yearling brown trout, and—in 1957—reduced the creel limit from ten to five trout.[54] By the late 1960s, when a four-mile section of the upper Battenkill in New York was being studied intensively, several things became apparent. Wild brown trout in this section, which are best adapted to stream life, were averaging almost an inch longer than the river's hatchery trout of similar age. More than two-thirds of the 10,500 hatchery yearlings being stocked were not being caught, which was a horrendous waste of money—hatchery trout are expensive. Anglers were catching few trout longer than a foot, such fish comprising only four percent of the total catch.

In response, stocking was stopped in this section, and more restrictive fishing rules were proposed. Wild-trout populations expanded to levels allowing about the same angler catch rates as before stocking was halted. The restrictive regulations took longer, finally being adopted after pressure from sportsmen's groups and some riparian landowners in 1971. Essentially the same rules have been in effect since that time: A three-fish creel limit and artificial-lures only. Kept trout must be at least ten inches long. The special-regulations section now extends from the state line downstream about four miles to the covered bridge at Eagleville. I've fished this stretch regularly since 1975, and the long-term effect of these rules is apparent: There are obviously more trout here than in most other river sections, and the fishing is that much better.

Brook-trout populations have apparently undergone a long-term decline in the same water, perhaps because of increased competition from greater numbers of brown trout. Because the brook trout, as an indigenous species, deserve some greater protection, placing brook trout under an even more restrictive catch limit would probably have some benefit. Also, the majority of brown trout here are relatively small, which I take to mean that a slot limit, similar to that recently proposed in Vermont to protect more desirable ten- to fourteen-inch trout, could also be beneficial. A Battenkill slot limit was proposed internally among New York's Inland Fisheries managers some years ago but was never adopted for reasons I've not been able to determine. The state's present policy seems to be benign neglect, enforced for the most part by tight state budgets. The current regulations are working to a degree, no one's complaining loudly, and well enough is let alone.

The balance of New York's Battenkill that offers good trout habitat—generally from Eagleville downstream to East Greenwich along Route 29—continues to be stocked annually with yearling brown trout. This seems to satisfy a political constituency that wants to dunk worms for skinny little hatchery fish next to highway bridges. This river section can and does support wild brown trout—including some very large ones—and stocking does absolutely nothing for the river, except perhaps to depress the numbers of wild fish. It is nothing more—or less—than politics.

In a program that apparently extends back to the 1930s, New York has been extraordinarily successful in obtaining deeded riverbank easements for fishing access along the Battenkill. With a few intermittent breaks, these easements exist on both sides of the river all the way from the state line to Greenwich some eighteen miles downstream. I won't take the space here to detail the individual easements, but it's generally safe to assume that as an angler you've got the right to walk up or down the riverbank for fishing unless the land is posted otherwise, which some of it is. This right of access does not pertain to casual hikers, boaters, swimmers, or picnickers, nor does it mean a fisherman can go traipsing across a newly planted cornfield to get to the river, which is rude as well as being bad public relations. Most such easements extend back thirty-three feet from the river's edge and can be reached from access areas posted as such by the state or from bridge crossings.

These same easements allowed a substantial program of physical stream improvement to be undertaken by New York during the late 1950s and 1960s. There are numerous log-cribbing wing dams and similar devices — designed to deflect the river's current and to maintain deep, fast channels — spread along the river from the state line several miles downstream to Shushan and beyond. These are of considerable benefit to landowners who granted angling easements because the devices have greatly curbed riverbank erosion and loss of land. New York, like most states, will not install such devices in locations without angling easements or other public access. Unfortunately, most of these devices were designed and installed before the importance of overhead cover became commonly known among fisheries managers. While they do deflect current and create deeper river channels for trout, they don't add as much overhead cover as devices of modern design and thus don't contribute as much as they might to increasing the river's overall trout population. Then, too, after twenty or thirty years, many of the instream devices installed by New York are starting to come apart, having been naturally eroded by the river. For the time being, at least, there's little if any money available for maintenance or improvement.

While New York has a long history of land acquisition for public benefit, similar programs have not been pursued to the same degree in Vermont. Now it may be too late. Land prices are rising while state budgets are shrinking, which makes state acquisition of access areas or easements difficult or impossible. Historically, Vermont fish and wildlife agencies have relied on the cooperation of private landowners in providing hunting and fishing access to unposted land and waterways. Fifty years ago, this worked adequately. But now it's be-

Fisherman and canoeists at West Arlington. The Battenkill's narrow channel frequently puts trout, fishermen, and floaters in the same spots...to the detriment of all three.

coming a rapidly increasing problem as some areas, such as the Battenkill, are becoming more intensively used and landowners are becoming less tolerant. Vermont owns only one angling-access easement along the Battenkill's riverbank — a two-mile stretch on the Hill Farm section in Sunderland. Traditional public access is gained at bridge crossings, by highway rights-of-way adjacent to the river, and by railroad rights-of-way also near the river, but all of these are open to future question as points of public access. With more fishermen, hikers, canoeists, inner-tube floaters, and others using the river every year, access will become increasingly difficult. Of the river's several upstream problems, future public access is by far the most significant.

Canoes. If you want to see a Battenkill trout fisherman get red in the face and start sputtering, that's all you have to say. Just one word. Canoes.

The Battenkill's gentle flow through miles of pastoral landscape makes it an ideal river for canoeing or drifting in an inner tube. During the past ten years, especially, the river has been discovered by canoeists and tubers, who are on the river in ever-increasing numbers between mid-May and early October and generally between Sunderland, Vermont, and Greenwich, New York. There are presently two canoe-rental outfitters on the river itself, and still other outfitters bring customers to the river on day trips. Local gas stations make extra money renting inner-tubes to flocks of floaters, and on many summer weekends some river sections acquire a carnival-like atmosphere. For floaters, it's wonderful. For fishermen, it's a disaster.

Because the waterway is essentially public, canoeists and tubers have the same rights as fishermen. The only exception is in the case of access or riverbank easements that are deeded for angling use only, but this technicality is little observed or enforced in either Vermont or New York. Because floaters scare the trout that fishermen are trying to catch, the two river uses are essentially incompatible, most especially as they both escalate. The problem on the Battenkill is acute because the river's channel is narrow, which means fishermen, trout, and floaters are all concentrated in the same spots; unlike, say, the big, 200-foot-wide Delaware River in New York where canoes and fishermen may be separated by a hundred feet or so when measured across the river's width.

Ten and twenty years ago the midday summertime fishing on the 'Kill between Sunderland and Shushan was excellent. The river stays naturally cold because of its springs, so the trout remained active in summer, rising sporadically all day long to ants and other terrestrial insects near the riverbanks. Such fishing no longer exists in much of the river; increased river traffic is the reason. Yes, you'll see a trout rise here and there on a July afternoon, but the same fish is being frightened into hiding every half hour or so by canoes or tubes floating overhead. The fishing suffers as a result, and many non-resident anglers who once traveled to the Battenkill in summer now avoid it for that reason.

The problem is most acute in West Arlington, where a lovely seven-mile river reach is the most popular section for both fishermen and floaters. While most canoeists and tubers are generally courteous — even if inept at such things as paddling and steering — the few exceptions have been like pouring gasoline on a brush fire. A couple of years ago one local landowner was punched after asking a tuber not to cross his land, an incident finally resolved with the help of a deputy sheriff. Joyce "Birdie" Wyman, Arlington's normally cheerful town clerk who lives along the river, once described the scene as being "like a Coney Island on the water. Sometimes there's tubes on the river as far as you can see in each direction, canoes flying around, hitting fishermen, tubers with beer coolers. It's sad."[55]

It is sad. And it's a mess that's only getting worse. The town of Arlington last year created a study committee to review the conflict and to see if any sort of management or control was possible. Although the study is ongoing at this writing, a draft report released in late 1992 tended to the conclusion that public education — primarily regarding manners on the river — is about all that can be done.

That same report also included the following, which raises some interesting questions:

> In regard to recreational use impacts on the fisheries, it does not appear that floating has an impact on the trout...Brown trout tend to be nocturnal, thus minimizing direct conflict with some of the daytime recreational uses.[56]

Not true! Several scientific studies have shown that brown trout of about twelve inches long or less, which means more than ninety

percent of the trout in such streams as the Battenkill, will actively
feed all day long during the summer if they are undisturbed.[57] It is
true that trophy-size browns tend to be largely nocturnal, but these
fish invariably comprise less than one percent of the total brown-trout
population.

A little stream ecology will make the importance of this more
clear. Aquatic insects are a primary food of trout less than a foot
long. In the spring, nearly mature aquatic insect larva and nymphs
arc abundant. By July, almost all of the large nymphs and larvae
have hatched as adults and are gone from the river. They are re-
placed by eggs and minuscule, newly hatched nymphs, which are too
small to be a significant trout food. So in summer trout turn to terrestrial insects; ants, beetles, and the like that have fallen in the river
and that at this season may comprise sixty percent or more of a
trout's diet.

Along comes a canoe or inner tube. The trout, now frightened,
stops feeding on drifting terrestrials and hides instead. After a while,
all is quiet, so the trout resumes feeding. Then another canoe. More
hiding. Then three inner tubes. More hiding. And so on until the
trout's normal summertime feeding behavior is totally disrupted by a
constant parade of floaters. The trout's body condition, meaning the
relation between girth and length, declines abnormally, which means
the fish is skinnier than normal. Reduced body weight usually tran-
slates into reduced fecundity; skinny brown and brook trout lay fewer
eggs when they spawn in the fall.

And so I believe the trout population *is* affected by intensive floating activity in rivers such as the Battenkill where a narrow channel
continually forces trout and floaters into the same locations. Some
people—both floaters and fishermen—will find all this a little farfetched, and it's true that my reasoning is only intuitive. To my
knowledge, there have never been any formal studies made on this
topic, comparing, for example, the physical condition of trout in a
river section with no floating to that in an identical (ideally, adjacent)
river section that's floated intensively. But the daytime behavior of
brown trout in summer has been well researched, and the inclination
of trout to hide when disturbed by floaters is obvious, especially in
the smooth, quiet flows of the Battenkill. An adverse effect seems
equally obvious.

State and local authorities will almost certainly be reluctant to regulate the floaters' right to use a public waterway by somehow restricting their numbers. But absent such regulation, the numbers of floaters will increase. In ten years there will be more canoes and inner tubes. In twenty years, even more. Without some kind of regulation, these private rights will continue to be loaded on the public back until — somewhere, somehow — it breaks. Lessons in stream manners — printed handouts and signs along the river — may alleviate things briefly, but don't address the long-term problem of growing numbers. If I ran the zoo, which obviously I don't, I would immediately restrict *all* floating — commercial and private — on the *entire* river to even- (or odd-) numbered days of every month from May through October. Enforcement would be required, but a single state officer — a part-time game warden, perhaps — could accomplish the job. Young local children with inner tubes — the favorite flag waved by the unrestricted-river-rights crowd — would simply be advised to swim without their tubes on certain days. Such a rule could be a start, giving both landowners and fishermen half a quiet summer instead of none.

In fairness, I have to point out that at least one of the canoe outfitters — Jim Walker of Battenkill Canoe — limits his customers' trips to between 9:30 A.M. and 5:30 P.M., which helps to keep the prime times of early morning and evening more open for fishermen. But a large part of the problem comes from independent floaters — a van full of kids, inner tubes, and cases of beer is a common example — who care about nothing more than having a good time. These sorts of user conflicts have become enormous problems on other rivers such as Maine's Saco, New York's Esopus, and Michigan's Au Sable. It will continue to get worse along the Battenkill, too, as numbers of floaters increase with each passing year. Conflicts will likewise escalate, especially with riparian land owners, and "posted" signs will start to proliferate. Any regulation of these competing uses within a public right seems not to be in the cards. The outlook is dismal.

CHAPTER 8

Fishing
the
'Kill

*T*his could be a suicide note or a love letter. I'm not sure which.

The Battenkill is more crowded with fishermen now than it was in 1975 when I first began fishing it regularly, and my suggesting places and ways in which more and larger trout can be caught here will only increase the crowding. In my own self interest, I should be describing mythical fish-kills, rampant water pollution, and stream banks littered with medical waste over which crawl numerous rattlesnakes. I've worried about that a great deal in thinking of this book and explained my concerns at length one morning to Carl Navarre, a neighbor, fisherman, and former publishing executive, during a chance encounter on the steps of our village general store.

"Don't worry about it," he finally said, smiling. "The kind of fishing you're describing is so demanding of patience that most people won't bother or be able to do it anyway." This was a shrewd observation and eased my mind a little. So I'll tell what I know — or much of it — while omitting a favorite tributary or two and a small handful of spots along the main river that I'll keep to myself for a while yet. I am most often a fly fisherman by choice, so most of this chapter concerns fly fishing on the 'Kill. To be fair to other fishermen, I've included some information on specialized lure and bait tactics near the chapter end. I'm also assuming that as a reader you've got some basic fly-fishing knowledge, gained from one of many short fly-fishing schools, perhaps, or a book, or just plain experience, allowing my use of jargon without endless explanation.

After about forty years of chasing trout from Maine to California and beyond, I know that the Battenkill is my favorite place. This might be true only because, among many other spots, I know it best. Certainly within rivers of my acquaintance the 'Kill is the prettiest. Its open meadows, gentle landscape, and clear pools seem in wonderful harmony with the valley's picturesque villages; all combining as an image of what a trout stream should be and all too seldom is. It is a pastoral picture seemingly re-created from Isaac Walton's 1653 *Compleat Angler*, in which he was as eloquent about the rural British countryside as about its fishing, although unlike Walton's enchanting tale I've seen no voluptuous milkmaids cavorting along the river.

The Battenkill is also among the most — if not *the* most — technically difficult fly-fishing stream in America. I say this not from some perverse hometown pride but from experience. The fishing in other American rivers famous for their demands on angling tactics — Fall River, Silver Creek, the Henrys Fork, Armstrong's, the Firehole, the Letort, the Beaverkill, or Housatonic — is relatively easy by comparison. Some fly fishermen will resent my having said this; most Battenkill veterans will agree with it. The late John Atherton, whose 1951 book *The Fly and the Fish* was largely based on his long Battenkill experience, called it "the most difficult of rivers and yet the most rewarding in the things which count the most."

Late in the 1970s, when Joan and the late Lee Wulff were moving from New Hampshire to New York's Beaverkill Valley to establish a fishing school, I asked Lee why they weren't going to the New York Battenkill instead, where Wulff had lived between 1940 and 1960 and where he still owned land. He gave a number of reasons, such as

Here I'm carefully stalking a quietly rising trout in the shallow tail of a West Arlington flat. The time is about nine P.M. in June; photographed with ultra-high-speed film. *Photo by Emily Merwin.*

The strike! The brown was a good one for this river, about sixteen inches. Trout rising gently in the tail shallows here are so predictable that I was able to set up a tripod-mounted camera and telephoto lens in the riffle downstream, hollering "shoot!" to my daughter at the right instant. *Photo by Emily Merwin.*

drawing students from the suburban New York market, among which was the obvious need for beginning students to be able to catch some trout. His beginners could catch at least a few Beaverkill fish, he said, but similar results with Battenkill browns would be almost impossible.

There are several reasons for this. The trout themselves are all wild, streambred fish by their very nature harder to catch than the hatchery trout to which many visiting fishermen are accustomed. The only exceptions are those brown trout stocked by New York in the lower river downstream of the special-regulations section, generally from Shushan downstream to the Route 22 bridge crossing and beyond. Here one can fish near the highway bridges where stocking is done and sometimes catch numerous seven- to eight-inch-long hatchery browns while using a Hornberg, Mickey Finn, or any other general attractor pattern to which such easily duped fish often respond. These same tactics work so seldom in the upstream wild-trout water as to be not worth trying, although fishermen accustomed to this sort of fishing often *do* try to their eventual frustration.

The Battenkill's wild brown and brook trout are also well educated and often exceptionally fussy as to fly pattern. This attribute isn't unique to the river, being common to many hard-fished trout streams, but it is part of the trout fishing equation here. Partly because of the Battenkill's longstanding reputation, and partly because of the nearby Orvis Company, there are numerous skilled fly fishermen living on or near the river, more than are found in actual residence near the Beaverkill or Housatonic, for example. Most of them fish the river regularly and release most of their fish. By the time one of the river's brown trout reaches age three and is about ten inches long, he or she has quite literally seen it all as far as fishing tactics are concerned. Interestingly, the Battenkill's larger brown trout, meaning those greater than fourteen inches long, when found (rarely) rising are usually easier to fool than smaller browns or brook trout that tend to be more fussy. I believe this is because the bigger browns rise much less frequently than smaller ones, and thus have less short-term experience with dry flies.

Trout in the Battenkill are also easily spooked. Sloppy wading, grinding gravel underfoot, slapping the water's surface with your line, and casting a careless shadow are among many things that send trout here darting for cover. Many fishermen are accustomed to hatchery fish that are in turn accustomed to and not bothered by human activity. Others frequent catch-and-release areas, such as on the Beaverkill, where many smaller trout develop a tolerance that allows a close approach with little care. Not so on the Battenkill, where bad habits acquired elsewhere just plain won't work. The wild trout on the 'Kill are just that — wild — and the fisherman who sloppily wades its quiet waters will frighten dozens of trout for every one he or she catches.

However, streambred, selective, and skittish trout are found in other rivers, too, and don't alone account for the Battenkill's widely known difficulty. Additional angling problems spring from the river's physical character. Because of its low gradient, much of the river is comprised of long, slow-flowing flat pools interspersed with short riffles. The bottom is generally composed of small stones, again because of the slow current, and there's very little cover for trout at midstream. Most trout most of the time are found along the banks, associated with larger rocks, half-sunken logs, or overhanging brush. Instead of being concentrated at the tumbling head of a pool — as is common in many rivers — the trout are strung out along the edges of a brushy flat that may be from one to two hundred yards long and often more. Here the slow-flowing water is clear, from a few inches to three feet deep, and here the trout hold with little effort. They have all the time in the world to carefully examine every tidbit — including your fly — as it floats slowly past.

The current often looks smooth and of consistent speed — perfect for dry-fly work — but it's not. First, the current near the bank is almost always slower than at midstream, so drag is an inevitable problem. Second, because of slight irregularities in the bottom, there usually are numerous intermittent and random whorls of current traveling from the bottom to the surface, where the whorls flatten, spread, and gradually disappear as their energy dissipates. This creates secondary surface currents of irregular and unpredictable speed that turn your drifting fly line into a writhing eel, with a dragging fly the result. I have seen this phenomenon on other rivers, but never to the same extent. Primary currents in other rivers seem either fast enough to make such secondary currents insignificant or slow enough so these current events occur seldom. On the Battenkill, secondary surface currents are a fly fisherman's nightmare, often requiring considerable skill to achieve drag-free floats.

The hatches are different, too. Because of the river's low gradient and generally slow flow, its streambed is relatively homogenous. Small, smooth stones ranging in size up to a softball are the most common bottom type while sand, silt, and beds of rotting leaves are found in the slower margins. Because the stream-bottom habitat is different than that of most other eastern trout streams, the aquatic-insect community is different, also. Slow currents, for example, favor clambering mayfly nymphs of the genera *Ephemerella, Baetis, Paraleptophlebia*, and *Pseudocloeon*, and some species of each are abundant in the Battenkill. The clinging nymphs of other, more rocky fast-water streams are scarce, and the Beaverkill's famous early-season hatches of Quill Gordons and other *Epeorus* mayflies are gen-

Tom Merwin with a big brown that took a Rusty Spinner on a foggy June morning.

erally absent here. March Browns, Gray Foxes, and other clinging *Stenonema* species are present, but only in limited numbers.

The slow, silty margins favor other clambering species as well and are textbook habitat for millions of *Tricorythodes* mayfly nymphs. These flies emerge on most mornings from mid-July through late September and are among the Battenkill's most prolific and productive hatches. Here also are found swimming mayfly nymphs typical of slow or still waters, notably *Siphlonurus quebecencis*, which is common and has the unusual (for a mayfly) habit of climbing above the water on an adjacent log or other object before emerging from its nymphal shuck. Its hatches are thus generally unimportant to fly fishermen, but spinner falls of the same species are very important in June. Other slow-water forms include various craneflies, the larvae of which are especially abundant at the bottoms of deep eddies in collections of dead leaves and silt. Among other bottom fauna are crayfish, which are fairly common and an important food source for larger brown trout.

Various stoneflies are present but aren't as abundant as they are in steeper, more tumbling rivers. Smaller forms such as the familiar pale-yellow *Isoperla* and pale green *Alloperla* flies are most common in riffle and fast-water areas. Burrowing mayfly nymphs are scarce because most of the bottom isn't suitable for their burrows. Big Yellow Drakes (*Ephemera varia*) hatch sporadically along the river shores in mid-June, and their rapidly swimming nypmhs occasionally draw slashing rises from larger fish. Cream Variants (*Potomanthus distinctus*) become increasingly common as one progresses downstream and are an excellent late June to mid-July late-evening hatch in some sections that often brings bigger fish to the surface. There is one short stretch of the lower river offering an excellent Brown Drake hatch (*Ephemera simulans*) typically at the end of May. Finally, large Mahogany Duns (*Isonychia bicolor*) seem to be increasingly common in areas of faster water. Fisherman commonly note this June hatch as being restricted to the lower river, but I've collected their nymphs in areas of fast water with a large-rubble bottom as far upstream as the East Dorset headwaters north of Manchester.

The Battenkill's caddisflies are both abundant and diverse, and my own catalog is still far from complete after fifteen years of casual collecting. The genus *Brachycentrus*, often called grannom or shadfly locally, is the best known of the 'Kill's many caddis and is a mid-May to June hatch. The insect's tan wings and light-green body are distinctive. There are abundant free-living *Rhyacophila* larvae in riffle sections, which are the green caddis worms found when rocks are overturned. Adults have dark olive-green bodies and are also a late May emergence. There's a medium-gray adult caddis common on the river in June, apparently of the *Psilotreta* genus, to which trout often become selective. All of the newly conventional caddis-emerger patterns will work at times as long as they reasonably match the naturals, but my favorite is the so-called Vermont Caddis, tied without a tail to hang suspended in the surface tension much like an emerging pupa. I usually use an Elkhair Caddis of appropriate size and color to imitate adults, but tie a specific imitation of the gray *Psilotreta* flies with down wings of gray hen-hackle tips that has proved more effective.

Terrestrial insects are important here from early May (carpenter ants) through the frosts of September. Small flying ants are common in autumn, and some of the most intense rises of trout I've seen here have been to afternoon ant swarms starting in late August. The ants are small, so check the water's surface carefully before choosing a pattern. Grasshopper and cricket imitations have proved less important here than on other rivers, but small beetle imitations sometimes work well. Ants, however, are by far the most important. Small, fur-bodied imitations seem to work best. I've had very poor luck here with the popular balsa-wood McMurray Ant pattern that works so well elsewhere.

It is common on the Battenkill to see the same trout rising sporadically, meaning once every ten or fifteen minutes, rather than the more frequent riseforms that occur during an intense insect hatch. Most of the river's fly hatches are intermittent for the better part of their duration, which may be as long as three or four hours, and the trout respond accordingly. This makes them harder to fool than fish that are rising avidly to a steady stream of insects riding the current. Because most hatches are less intense than on other streams, the fishing becomes more intense. Getting the right fly over a sporadically rising fish at the right time sometimes requires a great deal of patience.

Finally, and partly because swift, slow, and stillwater insect habitats are often adjacent in one section of river, masking hatches are common. In such cases, fish are feeding on the less apparent of two or more insect species that are active on or in the stream at the same time. Hendrickson (*E. subvaria*) and little Blue Quill (*Paraleptophlebia* sp.) mayflies hatch at the same time in early May, for example. Even though the 'Kill's Hendrickson hatch is famous, the trout sometimes forget this and feed avidly on the much smaller Blue Quills instead. This seemed especially prevalent last spring (1992) and frustrated a great many fishermen who didn't watch the river closely to see what was really happening.

Fly tackle for the Battenkill should be on the light side. You'll most often be fishing fairly small flies at distances of fifteen to sixty feet. I use an eight- to nine-foot graphite rod of medium action because accuracy and delicacy are at more of a premium than distance. Fast-actioned rods are more of a hindrance than a help. Four-weight rods are my current favorite. Lighter lines give me trouble in a breeze; heavier lines hit the 'Kill's quiet currents too hard. Because you'll most often be fishing with a 6X or lighter tippet, a better reel is helpful. Larger brown trout often run a considerable distance here when first hooked on a light leader, so you need a reel that will yield line smoothly under minimum tension. I use either my old, battered Hardy LRH or an Orvis CFO-III, both of which have smooth, double-pawl check systems that can be finely adjusted; there are few others that work as well.

Just about all of the common cautions and equipment advice generally applied to trout fishing apply here, including using waders with felt soles. The river bottom is quite clean, but still too slippery for sneakers. Because the 'Kill remains cold all summer, the warmth of neoprene waders is a plus. The river is more difficult to wade than it first appears, and often when quietly wading a long flat I've come to a suddenly deep section and extricated myself only with difficulty. The current, while smooth, "has a pretty good push to it," as my friend Dick Finlay likes to say. The problem increases when small bottom rocks start rolling underfoot, so be careful.

River sections between Manchester and Arlington tend to be crowded with alders and with steep, muddy banks that often drop directly into deep water. Getting in and out of the river is more difficult than in the more open sections of Arlington and downstream, but the

fishing is correspondingly better. Because this water is fished less frequently, paths to the river are few; the easiest access is usually by the
adjacent railroad tracks. The first time I tried this section, I fished until well after dark, unsuccessfully working over a pair of large browns
that were rising noisily in a long, still pool. The bank was a dark fea-
tureless thicket for as far as I could see, and I had no idea how to find
the path by which I'd entered. The alders, grapevines, and blackberry
bushes were so thickly intertwined where I attempted to leave the
river that progress was almost impossible. I wound up taking my rod
apart and crawling on hands and knees over roots and through the
darkness in what I knew to be the general direction of the railroad
tracks. After about twenty minutes of fumbling and quiet cursing, my
head bumped a solid object. A fence post. It took another half an
hour to negotiate the tangled fence and bushes until I emerged,
finally, on the railbed some seventy-five feet from the river. Once was
enough. I still sometimes fish the same water, but now tie a white
handkerchief to the alders where I enter the river from one of many
dim paths, making the way out easy to spot, even in darkness.

The Battenkill is foremost a dry-fly stream. While I and others
sometimes take a few fish with nymphs, wets, or streamers, the river's
smooth flow is best suited to surface work. There's no snobbery im-
plied here; dry flies and related emerger patterns simply are the most
effective way to fish this river most of the time for trout both large
and small.

Anglers new to the river — and even some stubborn old-timers —
make two common mistakes. The first is using too heavy a leader. Because getting drag-free drifts is a paramount problem in these tricky
and slow currents, use a three- to four-foot-long tippet of 6X (or
lighter with ultra-small flies) for *everything* except streamers, even if
the book you've read says to use 4X with your size-14 Hendrickson
dries. I only switch to a heavier tippet when using a large, air-resistant
fly or when the wind is blowing and accurate casting with a fine tippet
becomes impossible.

The other common problem is sloppy wading, and the importance
of this can't be overstated. The Battenkill's long, slow flats are most
rewarding of patience. Wade slowly, *make no ripples*, and take plenty
of time between steps. I often spend an hour, sometimes more, in

Casting to a rise during a mid-October afternoon hatch of minute Pseudocloeon mayflies on the lower river...

...and hooking a small brown trout.

wading only a hundred feet or so through one of these still flats, which drives some of my more impatient friends nuts. I also spend considerable time standing still in knee-deep water, waiting, and watching. Often, the reward comes in taking one or more browns of fourteen to eighteen inches long that eventually rise quietly in only inches of water along the bank. Visiting anglers almost never see such fish; hurried wading is almost always the reason why not.

After eighteen seasons here, I've settled into a pattern of fishing drys from a midstream position, casting slightly down and across-stream to the bank. The river is wide enough from Arlington down-stream to allow this method, which is both easier and generally more effective than struggling against the current and fishing drys in a tra-ditional, upstream manner. The usual variety of modern slack-line and reach casts work well when fishing down and across, and when a fly is refused, the current swings it to midstream where the cast can be retrieved without spooking bank-side fish. And wading gently with the current down a long flat causes fewer fish-scaring ripples than wading upstream.

Down-and-across dry-fly fishing also makes it relatively easy to work — rather than dead-drift — the fly. Although a drag-free drift is the first method of choice in covering a rising trout, twitching the fly slightly is often necessary to elicit a rise. This is especially true when fishing Elkhair Caddis patterns that should be twitched very slightly — only an inch or two — between brief dead-drift floats for best results. This is also the single best method of fishing the river blind, meaning in the absence of rising trout, after mid-May when the fish have become accustomed to seeing adult caddis. Work *slowly* along, casting a small size-eighteen dry caddis to the bank and punctuating its drift with brief, sharp twitches. The trout's response is often viol-ent, much like a largemouth bass exploding through the lily pads to take a surface plug. I once took three browns over sixteen inches plus several smaller trout — none of which I'd seen rising — in a single morning by this method from the big water below Shushan, which was my best Battenkill morning in fifteen years.

Thinking of the 'Kill's bigger downstream sections always reminds me of the Jesus Pool, a large, deep hole in a river section between Shushan and Rexleigh that's far from any road. Access to this area is by the New York State parking lot at Salem's Rexleigh Covered

Bridge off Route 22, and it's a three-mile hike on the old railroad tracks upstream along the river before the next road is reached. Pools here don't have widely accepted names and are usually located verbally with reference to one of four railroad bridges crossing the river in this stretch. The first time Bill Herrick and I approached one of these pools several years ago, we saw the surface roll of a brown trout so obviously huge that the expletive "Jesus!" was immediate, hence the name.

As far as I know, that big fish was hooked only once. The following May, my brother Tom Merwin and I were having a good morning on the lower river with numerous trout rising to spent Hendricksons. Morning spinner falls — often around 8:30 A.M. — are common on the 'Kill, especially if the previous evening has been stormy and the morning is calm. Reaching the appointed pool, we saw an obviously large trout rising steadily next to an old sycamore tree and just above where the pool's smooth flow broke into a riffle. Tom waded quietly into position while I waded upstream in the same run. After considerable silence, I heard an immense splash downstream, quickly followed by some loud cursing.

Jesus had risen. But the leader had failed. We never saw the Jesus fish again, although later in the summer and in the same pool, I watched Bill Herrick catch and release one of the apostles — a nineteen-inch brown that fell for a Cream Variant.

Spinner falls are exceptionally important on the Battenkill because so many of its mayfly hatches are sporadic. Many mayfly species that have emerged intermittently over a period of several days become concentrated on a few evenings when they return to the river in mating swarms. Sparsely tied mahogany or rusty spinners are basic equipment from mid-May through the summer in sizes 12 through 22. You'll also want a fairly large cream spinner, say #12, for summer spinner falls of *Potomanthus* flies, and some small, olive spinners in sizes 18 and 20.

The lower ends of long quiet pools are especially important at such times and in recent years have always provided, for me at least, the season's largest trout. This is particularly true in the still flats at West Arlington and downstream, where the largest browns rising at dark are usually in only inches of water, sipping spinners and making the merest of ripples in the slick tailouts. This is so predictable that I now wade slowly into position well ahead of time, and then stand still, waiting. The motionless wait is often an hour or more, and sometimes my legs cramp a little, but I've proved to myself many times that moving again — taking even one more step — will ruin an evening's fishing.

As dusk falls on a calm evening, mayfly spinners fall spent on the surface, and trout begin rising with increasing frequency. The small fish are most evident, rising at midstream and often just a few feet away if I remain motionless. It's tempting to cast to the fish but better to wait. In a little while I'll see a quiet rise near the bushes and perhaps the dorsal or tail fin of a much bigger trout at it turns down after rising. Now it's a short sidearm cast, dropping the little fly with a slack leader tippet just above the fish. A quiet wrinkle at the surface. Raise the rod to tighten gently. There's weight there; not just the scurry-up flipping of a little fish. The trout will run. You can count on that, so clear your line. Hopefully, you'll play the fish firmly but still gradually enough to minimize surface splashes and still without moving your feet.

On a good night, I'll take three or four browns from twelve to fifteen or sixteen inches by this method from the tail of any one of several hard-fished West Arlington flats. The essential ingredient is getting into position and then standing still for a long time, which most people will find intolerable. But this water is heavily fished, and those trout that are easily caught unfortunately are removed very quickly under the present general angling rules. Those remaining are extraordinarily shy, and it's taken me almost twenty years to learn to stand still enough long enough to catch them.

The passage of an evening canoe or a late flock of tubers ruins the whole business, of course. Smaller trout will resume rising within twenty minutes to half an hour; larger trout will not. I have often in recent years left the river in disgust on a June evening when, after an hour of stalking and waiting out the fish, a flotilla has passed through the pool. Some visiting fly fishermen with no conception of old-fashioned stream manners are almost as bad, wading into a pool where I'm standing, waving a cheery hello, and splashily spreading their ripples from bank to bank. If the offender seems young, inexperienced, and pleasant — as many are — I sometimes walk over for a visit, eventually explaining in a kind way about manners and not disturbing the water. But if the fisherman is an old-timer who apparently should know better, I most often just leave rather than throwing stones at the guy, which is what he deserves. There are more bad manners displayed on the 'Kill with each passing season; fly fishermen are most guilty of this, which is a new and disturbing trend.

Happily, some of the canoeists are learning, at least a little. Outfitters, too, are starting to offer some instruction so that if a canoe-rental paddler is capable of steering—which many aren't—the canoeists are apt to pass behind a fisherman rather than between the angler and the riverbank he's facing. I make a point of turning to thank such people, hoping to reinforce their behavior. At other times, when faced with a giggling gaggle of canoes coming down the river every way but upside down, the only choice is to retreat. Summer weekends and holidays are now impossible fishing times between Sunderland and Shushan, and the best answer is to head for the upper river near Manchester or the big water well below Shushan where canoeing and tubing are less prevalent.

Bait and lure fishing are local traditions on the Battenkill. I've tried both a few times myself, mainly to discover what works and what doesn't; but I still fish flies by choice. There are just a few men on the river who are highly adept with both bait and hardware. Most who sling a big nightcrawler or spoon lack the skill with either method to take larger trout consistently. Here are a few suggestions for neophytes who want to try either, which I give with some reluctance because many bait-caught trout are unavoidably killed regardless of the angler's intentions. My only hope is that at least some of the trout you take will be released, as I release many of mine for you.

Fishing here with worms in low, clear water is a waste of time. Almost all of the Battenkill's brook and brown trout will ignore worms until a heavy shower roils the river slightly, which is when worms work best. Small, fresh minnows are a better bait. Rigging and fishing these properly is a real art that you can learn from such references as *McClane's Standard Fishing Encyclopedia*. Fortunately for the Battenkill's sparse population of large brown trout, there are very few minnow artists on the river. There is one other natural bait

Baitfishing for brookies in both tributaries and the mainstream is a venerable
Battenkill tradition.

so devastatingly effective that its public description would stretch the limits of my conscience, so I'll quit.

I'll try to be more helpful with lures, if only because lure-hooked fish stand a much greater chance of survival when released than those taken on bait. From April through early May when the water's cold and the trout are staying deep, the most effective spinning lures are those that likewise run deep. Cast your Mepps, Roostertails, C. P. Swings, and other heavy-bodied spinners in the one-quarter to one-eighth-ounce range upstream in the chutes of rough water above big pools, and then retrieve slowly back along the bottom with the current. This method continues to work well into June, but as the water warms and trout become more aggressive, a small floating Rapala with a gold finish becomes the most effective lure. Fish upstream, casting close and parallel to overhanging brush along the bank. Retrieve the lure in erratic darts back downstream; don't worry about retrieving it too fast. When a big brown decides to hammer your little plug, you can't reel fast enough to take it away from the fish. Working the deep, fast chutes above big pools in this manner usually produces larger trout than you'll catch in the same fashion from the pools themselves. Dawn and dusk are the best times, but the same tactic will work all day to a lesser degree. A light spinning outfit with six-pound-test line works well in the early season and high water; four-pound-test is a better bet after mid-May.

Finally, if I had to bet on taking a really large brown trout from the Battenkill, I'd use a medium-size floating Flatfish carefully in the shallow *tail* of a big, deep pool between 4:00 A.M. and 6:00 A.M. on any day in July. This is a dark and dirty business. It's also the time of greatest feeding activity for the river's largest trout, meaning fish of two or three on up to eight or more pounds. The tail of a big pool, where the water is from three feet to a few inches deep, is where these unusual and rare fish do most of their hunting just before dawn and most actively in July. It is more like hunting than fishing, and you'll probably have the river all to yourself. Realizing that the huge wakes you're seeing in the dim light are actually trout and not big beaver can be very exciting. For a very few people, the experience is worth stumbling around in the dark through alder tangles and river muck. I've tried it enough to know I won't be joining you. I've also tried it enough to know that some of the old yarns about hooks

The author at work on the lower river. *Photo by Tom Merwin.*

bent straight and tackle smashed in a violent encounter can still come true.

Because the Battenkill is so cold and the June air sometimes muggy, there are a few early-summer nights when a dense mist forms over the river, clinging tightly to the surface and extending only a few feet above the water. You can see it gathering now over the black water where the air is thick and seems to flow downhill at the river's pace. In eighteen years here, I've never seen the trout rise on such a night. So let's quit fishing, and I'll add a footnote or two.

I am glad that you came to fish the 'Kill, and I hope you're not disappointed. I've had quite a few friends from out West come to visit and to fish, some of whom were disappointed at not finding musclebound browns on every pool corner as they sometimes find back home. But the Battenkill's not like that. Your average fish here will be eight or nine inches long and sometimes you'll be working hard to get even those. Yes, there are larger fish. I fish the 'Kill for parts of three or four days every week all season and have averaged one or two eighteen-inch fish a year as my biggest. The largest I've ever landed here was an even twenty; that was last year on a little Rusty Spinner dry.

No, it's not just the trout. You can catch more and bigger trout in Montana, pop a few beers at the Grizzly Bar, and listen to a honkytonk jukebox down by the Madison. It's a loose, fun, uninhibited kind of fishing. The Battenkill is more like Bach; with green hills, covered bridges, and white-clapboard villages forming the gently repeating steps of a sweetly insistent fugue in which rising trout play an occasional part. Perhaps you'll develop a taste for it. As I have.

Appendix A:
Special Fly Patterns

*M*ost modern, conventional trout flies will work on the Battenkill at one time or another, but as a general case smaller is better unless a specific hatch requires a large imitation. As general dry flies, meaning those I use without a hatch to match, my own favorites are an Adams, Red Quill, Rusty Spinner, and Black Fur Ant — all in size 20. Larger versions are easier to fish and will sometimes work, but smaller flies take more fish here more often, even large browns. Elkhair Caddis work well, either for rising fish or when fishing blind, but usually have to be twitched to elicit a rise. Compara-dun style drys work best for imitating larger mayflies, although other veterans here would give an edge to parachute- or thorax-style ties. Wets, nymphs, and streamers should also be on the small side, although dry-fly fishing is so much more effective that I'm almost always fishing dry from early May through mid-October.

There are a few special patterns that have either evolved along the river or have for some reason become associated with it. Most aren't standard patterns carried by fly shops, but all can be tied to order by any competent fly tier.

BADGER SPIDER

HOOK: Size 14–18, Mustad 94840 or equivalent

THREAD: Tan 6/0 nylon

TAIL: Silver-badger hackle fibers tied long

BODY: Gold tinsel

HACKLE: Silver badger, tied two hook-sizes oversize.

Spiders were favorites of the late John Atherton on the 'Kill during the 1940s and are still extremely effective. Adult craneflies are numerous on and along the river in June, and spider drys may represent their awkward, gangly flopping. Silver-badger hackle is scarce and hard to obtain, but worth the effort.

VERMONT CADDIS

HOOK: Size 16–20, Mustad 94840 or equivalent

THREAD: 6/0 nylon; color to match body

TAIL: None

BODY: Color to match caddis natural; usually tan or olive

WING: None

HACKLE: Brown and grizzly mixed; tied one hook-size undersize.

This caddis style emerged from the Anglers' Nook on the lower river at Shushan during the early 1970s. It can be coated with flotant and twitched on the surface in conventional fashion. Most effectively, it should be fished undressed, hanging vertically and partly awash in the surface tension like an emerging natural.

BROWN PARACHUTE

HOOK: Sizes 14–20, Mustad 94840 or equivalent

TAIL: Brown hackle fibers

BODY: Dark rusty red dubbing fur

WING: White calftail, tied upright as a single post

HACKLE: Brown, tied parachute.

Richard Norman first showed me this tie along the lower river during the 1970s. It serves the same function as a Rusty Spinner, but is much easier to see on the water because of the white-post wing.

BATTENKILL FLATS

HOOK: Sizes 12–20, Mustad 94840 or equivalent

TAIL: Pale dun hackle fibers, tied long and split spinner style

BODY: Stripped red quill

WING: None

HACKLE: Pale dun tied parachute using the hackle stem as a post.

This is essentially a style of spinner pattern made popular locally by the late Dudley Soper, a wonderful man who was a fixture on the lower river through the early 1970s. Often made with other body and hackle colors, Soper called his wingless parachutes dime flats, nickel flats, and so on according the size of their radial hackle. The flies are hard to make, but devastatingly effective on trout sipping in slow, clear water. Richard Norman first showed me this red-quill version.

TRICO PARACHUTE

HOOK: Sizes 20–26, Mustad 94859 or equivalent

THREAD: Black 6/0 nylon

TAIL: Pale dun hackle fibers

BODY: Black dubbing fur tied sparse

WING: Pale gray polypropylene yarn tied as an upright post

HACKLE: Pale dun, tied parachute.

I first tied this style in the late 1970s after fussing with endless versions to imitate the 'Kill's abundant *Tricorythodes* mayfly hatches in summer. It continues to outperform any other style I've tried, including conventional spent ties as well as thorax versions.

BREADCRUST

HOOK: Sizes 12–18, Mustad 3906 or equivalent

THREAD: Orange 6/0 nylon

BODY: Orange floss over which is closely wrapped a section of quill stripped from a ruffed grouse tail feather, from which the hackle fibers have been roughly trimmed. The orange floss should be barely visible.

HACKLE: Grizzly hen.

This wet fly has long been associated with the Battenkill, although after many years of questioning I've yet to find out why. It did not originate here. Most versions show too much orange. The overall effect should be that of a dull brown body with just a hint of orange showing.

BROWN BOMBER

HOOK: Sizes 12–18, Mustad 3906 or equivalent

THREAD: Brown 6/0 nylon

TAIL: None

BODY: Gray muskrat-fur dubbing

HACKLE: Brown-mottled grouse or hen hackle.

During the 1940s and 1950s when fishing a multiple wet-fly cast was still common on the 'Kill, a Brown Bomber on the point with a Breadcrust dropper was the killing combination for brown trout in the lower river. It still works.

SHUSHAN POSTMASTER

HOOK: Sizes 6–10, Mustad 9575 or equivalent

TAIL: Brown-mottled turkey fibers tied short

BODY: Light yellow floss

RIBBING: Flat gold tinsel

THROAT: Red hackle fibers

WING: Fox squirrel tail fibers extending to end of tail.

The late Lew Oatman's famous pattern, named after Al Prindle, an enthusiastic fisherman who was also the postmaster at Shushan on the lower river during the 1930s and 1940s.

BATTENKILL SHINER

HOOK: Sizes 6–10, Mustad 9575 or equivalent

TAIL: Gray hackle fibers

BUTT: A few turns of red floss

BODY: White floss

RIBBING: Flat silver tinsel over white floss only

THROAT: Gray hackle fibers

WING: Two medium-blue saddle hackles under two silver-badger saddle-hackle feathers.

Another Oatman pattern and still my favorite streamer pattern for the 'Kill.

Some proven Battenkill flies. Top row: Vermont Caddis, Trico Parachute, Brown Bomber. Second row: Breadcrust, Shushan Postmaster. Third row: Battenkill Shiner, Brown Parachute. Bottom row: Badger Spider, Battenkill Flats.

Appendix B:
Aquatic-Insect Hatches

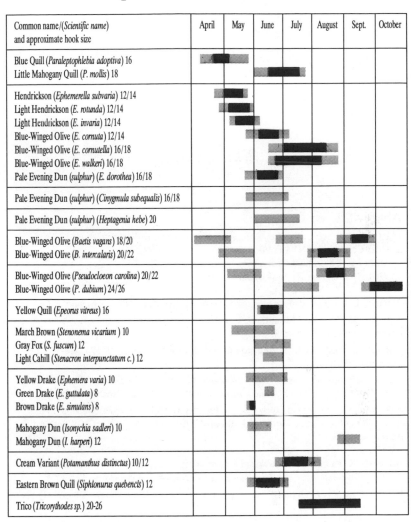

Common name/(*Scientific name*) and approximate hook size	April	May	June	July	August	Sept.	October
Blue Quill (*Paraleptophlebia adoptiva*) 16 Little Mahogany Quill (*P. mollis*) 18							
Hendrickson (*Ephemerella subvaria*) 12/14 Light Hendrickson (*E. rotunda*) 12/14 Light Hendrickson (*E. invaria*) 12/14 Blue-Winged Olive (*E. cornuta*) 12/14 Blue-Winged Olive (*E. cornutella*) 16/18 Blue-Winged Olive (*E. walkeri*) 16/18 Pale Evening Dun (*sulphur*) (*E. dorothea*) 16/18							
Pale Evening Dun (*sulphur*) (*Cinygmula subequalis*) 16/18							
Pale Evening Dun (*sulphur*) (*Heptagenia hebe*) 20							
Blue-Winged Olive (*Baetis vagans*) 18/20 Blue-Winged Olive (*B. intercalaris*) 20/22							
Blue-Winged Olive (*Pseudocloeon carolina*) 20/22 Blue-Winged Olive (*P. dubium*) 24/26							
Yellow Quill (*Epeorus vitreus*) 16							
March Brown (*Stenonema vicarium*) 10 Gray Fox (*S. fuscum*) 12 Light Cahill (*Stenacron interpunctatum c.*) 12							
Yellow Drake (*Ephemera varia*) 10 Green Drake (*E. guttulata*) 8 Brown Drake (*E. simulans*) 8							
Mahogany Dun (*Isonychia sadleri*) 10 Mahogany Dun (*I. harperi*) 12							
Cream Variant (*Potamanthus distinctus*) 10/12							
Eastern Brown Quill (*Siphlonurus quebencis*) 12							
Trico (*Tricorythodes sp.*) 20-26							

This chart is restricted to mayfly hatches; caddisflies are described within Chapter 8. Emergence dates and durations are approximate and may vary by as much as two weeks according to such things as depth of winter snowpack and long-term variations from normal, seasonal air temperatures. Not all the mayflies indicated are found in equal abundance every season and many are found only in specific sections of river according to habitat preferences unique to each species. The best reference by far for anglers wanting more information on the life histories of these and other mayflies is Fred Arbona's book, *Mayflies, The Angler, and The Trout* (New York: Lyons & Burford, 1989).

179

Bibliography

Abbreviations:
1. RC/AL: Russell Collection/Arlington, VT, Library.
2. CPL: Cambridge (NY) Public Library.
3. MSL: Mark Skinner Library, Manchester, VT
4. BML: Bennington (VT) Museum Library

ALDRICH, L. C., *History of Bennington County, Vt.* Syracuse, NY: D. Mason & Co., 1889.

AMBROSE, J., "Men and Mountains: Carl Ruggles, Vermont Composer." *Vermont History* 56 (1988): 4:230–239.

Anonymous, "Editorial." *Washington County* (NY) *Post*, April 29, 1937 [re: trout stocking in Battenkill].

_____., *History and Biography of Washington County and the Town of Queensbury, N. Y., with Historical Notes on the Various Towns.* New York: Gresham Publ. Co., 1894.

Arlington (Vt.) Battenkill Study Committee, "Battenkill Management Study: An Assessment of Use and Conflict. (draft copy)" Arlington, VT: Town of Arlington, November 1992.

BACHMAN, R., "Foraging behavior of free-ranging wild and hatchery brown trout in a stream." *Transactions of the American Fisheries Society* 113 (1984): 1–32.

BARNES, J. K., *Asa Fitch and the Emergence of American Entomology.* Albany, NY: NYS Museum Bull. No. 461, 1988.

BASSETT, T. D. S., ed., *Outsiders Inside Vermont.* Brattleboro, VT: Stephen Greene Press, 1967.

Beers, F. W., *Atlas of Bennington County, Vermont.* New York: F. W. Beers, 1869. (Reprint: Rutland, VT: Chas. Tuttle, 1969.)

Bennington County (Vt.) Regional Commission. "The Battenkill Study." Arlington, VT, 1986.

BIGELOW, E. L., and N. H. Otis, *Manchester, Vermont: A Pleasant Land Among the Mountains.* Manchester, VT: Town of Manchester, 1961.

BIGGENS, R. G., "Battenkill Creel Census: Job Progress Report: January 1, 1975–December 31, 1975." North Springfield, VT: Vermont Dept. of Fish and Wildlife, 1976.

_____., "Battenkill Fish Population Report: Job Progress Report, January 1, 1974 through December 31, 1974." North Springfield, VT: Vermont Dept. of Fish and Wildlife, 1975.

_____., "Fish Population Studies [Battenkill]: July 1, 1972–June 30, 1973." North Springfield, VT: Vermont Dept. of Fish and Wildlife, 1973.

_____., "Fish Population Studies [Battenkill]: July 1, 1971 to June 30, 1972." North Springfield, VT: Vermont Dept. of Fish and Wildlife, 1972.

_____., "Battenkill Stream Stocking Survey." North Springfield, VT: Vermont Dept. of Fish and Wildlife, 1969.

BOXALL, B., "Act 250 Commissioners Approve Plans for 120 Equinox Condominiums." *Bennington* (Vt.) *Banner*, May 28, 1981.

CALABI, S., "Trout 129, Dredgers O." *Manchester* (Vt.) *Journal*, Sept. 17, 1981.

CALLOWAY, C. G., *The Western Abenakis of Vermont, 1600–1800*. Norman, OK: Univ. of Oklahoma Press, 1990.

_____., "The Conquest of Vermont: Vermont's Indian Troubles in Context." *Vermont History* 52 (1984): 161–79.

Clearwater Chapter, Trout Unlimited, "An Angler's Guide to the Battenkill in New York State." Albany, NY: Clearwater Ch. T. U., 1983.

CONGDON, H. W., *The Covered Bridge*. (5th ed.) Middlebury, VT: Vermont Books, 1989.

CORAY, A., *Gazetteer of the County of Washington, N.Y., Comprising a Correct Statistical and Miscellaneous History of the Several Towns from their Organization to the Present Time*. Schuylerville, NY: (no publisher stated), 1849, 1850. [BML]

COSTELLO, F. J., "Report of Investigation of Arlington Gravel Bar." Montpelier, VT: Agency of Environmental Conservation, Dept. of Water. Res. and Env. Eng., 1981.

COX, K., "Battenkill Trout Population Assessment; July 1, 1991–June 30, 1992." North Springfield, VT: Vermont Dept. of Fish and Wildlife, 1992a.

_____., "Battenkill Trout Population Assessment: July 1, 1990–June 30, 1991." North Springfield, VT, Vermont Dept of Fish and Wildlife, 1991.

_____., "Proposed test-water program for quality trout management in the lower Battenkill." [re special regulations] North Springfield, VT: Vermont Dept. of Fish and Wildlife, 1992b.

_____., "Executive Summary: Proposed Test Water Program for Quality Trout Management in the Lower Battenkill." North Springfield, VT: Vermont Dept. of Fish and Wildlife, 1992c.

_____., "Draft Project Proposal: Battenkill Trout Habitat Enhancement and Streambank Stabilization Project." North Springfield, VT: Vermont Dept. of Fish and Wildlife, 1990.

_____., "Battenkill Voluntary Creel Survey: July 1, 1985 to June 30, 1986." North Springfield, VT: Vermont Dept. of Fish and Wildlife, 1986.

CRABTREE, P., "River Users Asked for Input on Management of Battenkill." *Rutland* (Vt.) *Daily Herald* November 11, 1992.

CRONON, W. *Changes in the Land: Indians, Colonists, and the Ecology of New England.* New York: Hill & Wang, 1983.

DILLON, J., "Ethan Allen Letter Sheds New Light." *Rutland* (Vt.) *Daily Herald*, October 14, 1990.

FISHER, D. C., *Vermont Tradition.* New York: Little, Brown, 1953.

FITCH, A., "Early History of the Town of Salem [NY]." Salem, NY: *The Salem Press*, 1927. [Written ca. 1850 and reprinted; ref. Salem, NY, Public Library. *The Salem Press* is long defunct.]

GRAHAM, H., "The Old Indian Trail Along the Battenkill River." unpubl. ms., [RC/AL]

GRAFFAGNINO, J. K., "Zadock Thompson and The Story of Vermont." *Vermont History* 47 (1979):4:237–257.

———., "Walter Hard's Vermont." *Vermont History* 49 (1981): 2:97–116.

———., "The Vermont 'Story': Continuity and Change in Vermont Historiography." *Vermont History* 46 (1978): 2:77–99.

GRUN, B. (trans.). *The Timetables of History.* New York: Simon & Schuster, 1991.

HALLOCK, C., "The Ondawa." *American Angler* September 25, 1886.

HAVILAND, W. A., and M. W. Power, *The Original Vermonters: Native Inhabitants Past and Present.* Hanover, NH: University Press of New England, 1981.

Hemingway, S., "Battenkill's Title May Lead to River's Fall." *Burlington* (Vt.) *Free Press* February 17, 1991.

HEINEL, T., C. Acton, and T. Hopkins, "Battenkill Water Quality Surveillance Project." (unpubl. ms.) Manchester, VT: Burr and Burton Seminary, 1988.

HERRINGTON, B. M., "Two-Hundredth Anniversary Address...[re. Cambridge, NY]." unpubl. ms., 1969. [RC/AL]

HEWITT, P. C., *The Geology of the Equinox Quadrangle and Vicinity, Vermont.* Montpelier: Vermont Development Department, Vermont Geological Survey Bull. No. 18, 1961.

JAMESON, J. F., *Narratives of New Netherland: 1609–1664.* New York: Scribners, 1909.

Jellison, C. A., *Ethan Allen: Frontier Rebel.* Syracuse: Syracuse Univ. Press, 1969.

JENKINS, T., "Social structure, position choice, and distribution of two trout species [brown and rainbow] resident in mountain streams." *Animal Behavior Monographs* 2(2) (1969): 57–123.

JOHNSON, C., *History of Washington County, New York.* Philadelphia: Everts and Ensign, 1878.

JOHNSON, C. W., *The Nature of Vermont*. Hanover, NH: University Press of New England, 1980.

KRESS, R. F., "Hatching Guide to the Battenkill." Manchester, VT: American Museum of Fly Fishing, 1991.

LANTIEGNE, E. L., "A History of the Fish Management Program on the [NY] Battenkill." Warrensburg, NY: Region Five, Bureau of Inland Fisheries, NYS Dept. of Env. Cons., 1976.

_____., "Angler Use of the Special Regulation Area of the Battenkill in 1973 and the Effect of Special Regulations on the Brown Trout and Brook Trout Populations." Warrensburg, NY: Region Five, Bureau of Inland Fisheries, NYS Dept. of Env. Cons., 1974.

_____., "The Effect of Two Years of Special Regulations on the Battenkill Trout Fishery." Warrensburg, NY: Region Five, Bureau of Inland Fisheries, NYS Dept. of Env. Cons., 1972.

_____., "Battenkill Creel Census Brief." Warrensburg, NY: Region Five, Bureau of Inland Fisheries, NYS Dept. of Env. Cons., 1969.

LEDLIE, D., "Dry flies on the Ondawa: The tragic tale of John Harrington Keene." [two parts] *The American Fly Fisher* 13 (1986): 1:8–17, and 13:2:9–17.

LORD, R., "The Vermont Test Water Study: 1935–1945 Inclusive." Montpelier, VT: Vermont Fish and Game Service Fish. Res. Bull. 2, 1946.

LOSSING, B. J., *The Hudson: From the Wilderness to the Sea*. Troy, NY: H. B. Nims & Co., 1866.

LUZADER, J., *Decision on the Hudson: The Saratoga Campaign of 1777*. Washington, DC: National Park Service, 1975.

MAFFLY, B., "River Hearing Switches Focus." *Bennington* (Vt.) *Banner* July 19, 1991.

MANN, Chester. *Jester Men*. Albany, NY: Weed-Parsons, 1909. [MSL] (Chester Mann is possibly a pseudonym for George Thatcher. The book is an anecdotal account of Manchester, VT, ca. 1900.)

MARSH, G. P., "Report, on the Artificial Propagation of Fish, made under the authority of the Legislature of Vermont." Burlington, VT, 1857. [RC/AL]

_____., *Man and Nature*. New York: Scribners, 1864. (Reprint, with annotations: D. Lowenthal, ed., Cambridge, Mass., Belknap/Harvard, 1965.)

McFADDEN, J., and E. COOPER. "An ecological comparison of six populations of brown trout." *Transactions of the American Fisheries Society* 91 (1962): 53–62.

MACFARLANE, R. M. F., 1986. "PFR maps—Battenkill (Washington County [NY])" Warrensburg, NY: NYS Dept. of Env. Cons. internal memorandum [detailing angling-access easements on the lower Battenkill].

McHENRY, S. G., "Vermont's Sleepy Hollow: The Colonial Dutch Landscape Legacy." *Vermont History*: 47 (1979): 4:279–285.

McMenemy, J., "Battenkill Creel Survey, Job Performance Report: July 1, 1988 to June 30, 1989." North Springfield, VT: Vermont Dept. of Fish and Wildlife, 1990a.

———., "Beebe Pond, Bennington County; Job Performance Report." North Spring field, VT: Vermont Dept. of Fish and Wildlife, 1990b.

———., "Branch Pond, Bennington County; Job Performance Report." North Springfield, VT: Vermont Dept. of Fish and Wildlife, 1990c.

———., "Bourn Pond, Bennington County; Job Performance Report." North Springfield, VT: Vermont Dept. of Fish and Wildlife, 1990d.

Mease, S., "Has the Cat Come Back?" *Vermont Life* 47 (1992): 2:30–34.

Meeks, H. A., *Time and Change in Vermont*. Chester, CT: Globe Pequot, 1986.

Miller, W. W., "Battenkill Fishery Overview." Warrensburg, NY: Region Five, Bureau of Inland Fisheries, NYS Dept. of Env. Cons., 1982.

———., "1968–1977 Battenkill Special Regulation Area Study Brief." Warrensburg, NY: Region Five, Bureau of Inland Fisheries, NYS Dept. of Env. Cons., 1978.

Montgomery, M. R., "Battenkill: Stream of Broken Dreams." *Glens Falls Post-Star* May 25, 1989.

Newton, E., *The Vermont Story*. Montpelier, VT: Vermont Historical Society, 1949.

O'Connor, K., "State Secession? Get Ready for the Great Debate." *Rutland* (VT) *Daily Herald* March 1, 1990.

Otis, J. C., Jr., "A Biological Survey of the Battenkill River System." Montpelier, VT: VT Fish and Game Service Bull. No. 27., 1941.

Page, J., "The Economic Structure of Society in Revolutionary Bennington." *Vermont History* 49 (1981): 2:69–84.

Pyne, L., "Battenkill banks get helping hand." *Burlington* (VT) *Free Press* Oct. 18, 1992.

Quinn, P., "Seeking Solutions to Battenkill Problems." *Manchester* (VT) *Journal* Nov. 18, 1992.

———., "Saving the River by Stewardship." *Manchester* (VT) *Journal* Nov. 18, 1992.

———., "Jury Out on Dorset Housing Proposal." *Manchester* (VT) *Journal* Sept. 30, 1992.

Randolph, J., "Battenkill Channelization Project May Turn Trout Haven into a Ditch." *Bennington* (VT) *Banner*, June 5, 1979.

———., "Report on the Battenkill." *Bennington* (VT) *Banner*, April 2, 1981.

———., "Dredging the Battenkill River." *Bennington* (VT) *Banner*, March 3, 1981.

Raymond, R. W., "Covered Bridges in the Cambridge District." *Old Cambridge: 1788–1988* Cambridge, NY: Towns of Jackson and White Creek, 1988.

REBEK, A., "The Selling of Vermont: From Agriculture to Tourism, 1860–1910." *Vermont History* 44 (1976): 1: 14–27.

RESCH, T., *Dorset: In the Shadow of the Marble Mountain*. Dorset, VT: Dorset Historical Society, 1989.

REZENDES, P. *Tracking and the Art of Seeing*. Charlotte, VT: Camden House, 1992.

ROCKWELL, N., *Norman Rockwell: My Adventures as an Illustrator*. Garden City, NY: Doubleday, 1960.

RODERICK, M., "Arlington Officials Seek Solutions to Gravel Bank Problem." *Bennington* (VT) *Banner*, July 10, 1981.

ROOMET, L. B., "Vermont as a Resort Area in the Nineteenth Century." *Vermont History* 44 (1976): 1: 1–13.

RUTTENBER, E. M., "Indian Geographical Names," in *Proceedings of the New York State Historical Association*. Albany, NY: 1906. [CPL]

SADLIER, R., and P. SADLIER, *Fifty Hikes in Vermont*. Somersworth, NH: NH Publ. Co., 1974.

SCHLESINGER, A. M., Jr., ed., *The Almanac of American History*. New York: Putnam, 1983.

SCHULLERY, P., "The Battenkill." *Vermont Magazine* September 1990: 37–39, 70–73.

Schupp, B. D., "Fishery Inventory Survey Report: The Lower Battenkill." Warrensburg, NY: Region Five, Bureau of Inland Fisheries, NYS Dept. of Env. Cons., 1976.

SCHWEIKER, R., *Canoe Camping Vermont and New Hampshire Rivers*. Somersworth, NH: NH Publ. Co., 1977.

SEVERANCE, C. R., and E. LANTIEGNE, "A Study of the Battenkill for Inclusion into the New York State Wild, Scenic, and Recreational Rivers System." Warrensburg, NY: Region 5, NYS Dept. of Env. Cons., 1974.

SEYMOUR, F. C., *The Flora of Vermont* (4th ed.). Burlington: Univ. of Vt. Ag. Exp. Sta. Bull. 660, 1969.

SHEDD, W., "Saving the Taconics." *Vermont Life* 47 (1992): 2:24–29.

SLAYTON, T., "The Battenkill: Troubled Beauty." *Rutland* (VT) *Daily Herald*, April 19, 1981.

SMITH, R., "What Makes the Battenkill So Special?" *Bennington* (VT) *Banner* Nov. 24, 1990.

———., "River Statute Complicates Erosion-Control Efforts." *Bennington* (VT) *Banner* Nov. 24, 1990.

STANLEY, P., "Angry Residents Want River Hearing Held in Arlington." *Bennington* (VT) *Banner* July 5, 1991.

SWIFT, E. M., *Vermont Place Names*. Brattleboro, VT: Stephen Greene Press, 1977.

TALLEUR, R., "Battenkill: River of Intimidation." *Fly Fishing Heritage* 2 (1989): 1:69–72.

THERRIEN, J., "Reports on Battenkill to get Public Review." *Bennington* (VT) *Banner* November 11, 1992.

Thompson, H. W., *New York State Folktales, Legends and Ballads*. New York: Dover, 1967.

Van Diver, B. B., *Roadside Geology of Vermont and New Hampshire*. Missoula, MT: Mountain Press, 1987.

————., *Rocks and Routes of the North Country, New York*. Geneva, NY: Humphrey Press, 1976.

U.S. Fish and Wildlife Service, "Endangered and threatened wildlife and plants." Washington, DC: Dept. of Interior, August 29, 1992.

Vermont Dept. of Fish and Game, "Annual Report." Montpelier, VT, 1922.

Vermont Dept. of Fish and Wildlife, "Vermont's Moose Status: 1991." Waterbury, VT: 1991.

Washington County (NY) Planning Department, *An Introduction to Historic Resources in Washington County, NY* (2nd. ed.). Ft. Edward, NY: Washington County Board of Supervisors, 1976, 1984.

Williams, H., *The Salem Book: Records of the Past and Glimpses of the Present*. Salem, NY: Salem Review-Press, 1956.

Wrenn, T., and E. Mulloy, *America's Forgotten Architecture*. New York: Pantheon, 1976.

End Notes

CHAPTER 1

1. *Washington County Post*, April 29, 1937. A complete run of this newspaper is on microfilm at the Cambridge (N.Y.) Public Library.

2. See Resch (1989).

3. The West Branch does *not* begin by flowing south from Prentiss Pond near Dorset's Church Street, as commonly reported. This pond drains entirely north into the Mettowee River system. The West Branch begins in the swamp some yards south of the pond where an almost imperceptible rise in the mushy landscape separates the drainage areas.

4. Most of this biographical information is derived from David Ledie's exceptional biography of Keene as published by The American Museum of Fly Fishing. See Ledlie (1986).

CHAPTER 2

5. Hall's willful destruction of Emmons' work was never proven. Their enmity is historical fact, as was Hall's presence on the same boat containing Emmons' shipment, which shipment never reached its destination. See, especially, Barnes (1988).

6. This account of the region's geology is derived from several sources, with those by Van Diver (1976, 1987) being the most helpful. See also Johnson (1980), which is less technical, and Hewitt (1961), which is extremely technical, among others.

7. One billion meaning one-thousand million.

8. These are average annual data for 1983. One measurement made in the summer of 1990 showed a pH of 4.41, which is dangerously low in terms of the pond's ecology and its ability to sustain brook trout. See McNemeny (1990da).

9. See, for example, McFadden and Cooper (1962), who describe one experiment that attempted to find a correlation between alkalinity and brown-trout growth in several streams, but which found instead that the connection was at best fuzzy.

10. For a more complete review of acid precipitation's effect on aquatic environments in general and on trout in particular, see my recent book *New American Trout Fishing*, and also Bob Boyle's book *Acid Rain*.

11. See Van Diver (1987).

12. See, for example, Johnson (1980).

CHAPTER 3

13. See, expecially, Cronin (1983).

14. Appearing in Jameson (1909).

15. Possibly remnant populations of eastern woodland elk or caribou, both of which soon became extinct regionally. He might also mean here moose meat, brought to the Hudson by Indians from the Green Mountain high country.

16. Fisheries managers in both Vermont and New York will take strong exception to this statement, even though current angling regulations in both states have been thoughtlessly structured to favor non-native species. This is explored at greater length in Chapter 7.

17. I have assumed the "Miss," because it better fits my image of the quaint, female Victorian botanist. I don't know whether or not she was in fact married.

18. See Rezendes (1992). This figure is about 10 pounds heavier than western coyotes.

CHAPTER 4

19. The best modern references I've found on early Native American activity in this region are Calloway (1990), and Haviland and Power (1981), both of which have excellent bibliographies.

20. See Calloway (1990).

21. Calloway (1990).

22. As quoted by Jellison (1969).

23. Jellison (1969).

CHAPTER 5

24. From Johnson (1878).

25. See Meeks (1986).

26. From Marsh (1864, 1965).

27. From Resch (1989).

28. Brook trout are unique among toutlike fishes in often deliberately selecting for spawning areas of streambed gravel with upwelling groundwater.

29. According to historian Marcus Cunliffe, appearing in Schlesinger (1986).

30. At Battenville, on the river in Greenwich, New York, in the 1830s.

31. As quoted in Barnes (1988).

32. From Barnes (1988).

33. So called because it occupies a triangular point of land between the Battenkill and Black Creek along Route 29 where Fitch's house still stands.

34. Romet (1976).

35. There are several large limestone caves in the upper valley. They are all unmarked with small entrances. They are also extremely dangerous, and for that reason I've omitted their locations or descriptions from this book.

36. As quoted by Otis (1961).

37. The most complete account of Charles Orvis and the evolution of The Orvis Company appears in *The Orvis Story* by Paul Schullery and Austin Hogan (1980), a company history commissioned and published by that Orvis to mark its 125th anniversary.

CHAPTER 6

38. The book is *Jester Men*, written under the pseudonym "Chester Mann." That the author was in fact George Thatcher is speculative and has never been firmly established.

39. These panels, with their numerous nineteenth-century photographs and flies, are in dire need of professional conservation and restoration. The American Museum of Fly Fishing staff tells me the panels have been reviewed by conservators from the Williamstown (Mass.) Regional Art Conservation Laboratory and that the museum is now looking for donors to cover the considerable expense of professional care. The panels are among the foremost artifacts of American angling history, so here's a plea for help. Contact the museum at Box 42, Manchester, VT 05254.

40. Hallock (1886).

41. See Williams's *The Salem [N.Y.] Book*, p. 216.

42. There's almost a complete set of these reports dating from the 1870s to the 1960s in the Russell Collection of Vermont material at the Canfield Library in Arlington.

43. That two different brown-trout strains are known to have been stocked here is significant. First, this provided the genetic diversity among individual brown trout necessary for quick adaptation to a new environment. Second, naturally reproducing brown trout here may eventually evolve as two distinct forms, each reflecting its unique and original European attributes.

44. G. Russell scrapbook No. 26, p. 36. Russell Collection, Canfield Library, Arlington, Vt. The clipping is dated, but the newspaper isn't identified.

45. Meyer (1981).

46. Rockwell (1960).

47. Ibid.

48. See Merwin, ed. (1989), p. 117. I never was able to find out just who Wulff meant by "we."

CHAPTER 7

49. See Talleur (1989).

50. See Cox (1991).

51. The Wisconsin experience is well-known, particularly as described in technical papers by Robert L. Hunt, which are cited elsewhere in numerous bibliographies so I haven't listed them here.

52. As cited in Dillon (1990).

53. See Lord (1946). Lord's data and modern survey data show a similar catch rate, but were established through different survey methods and are technically, at least, not directly comparable.

54. See Lantiegne (1976).

55. As quoted in Hemingway (1991).

56. From Arlington (Vt.) Battenkill Study Committee draft report; November 1992.

57. See, specifically, Bachman (1984) and Jenkins (1969).